Career Advising

Virginia N. Gordon

Career Advising

An Academic Advisor's Guide

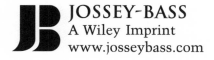

JOSSEY-BASS
A Wiley Imprint
www.josseybass.com

Published by Jossey-Bass
A Wiley Imprint
989 Market Street, San Francisco, CA 94103-1741   www.josseybass.com

Jossey-Bass books and products are available through most bookstores. To contact Jossey-Bass directly call our Customer Care Department within the U.S. at 800-956-7739, outside the U.S. at 317-572-3986, or fax 317-572-4002.

Jossey-Bass also publishes its books in a variety of electronic formats. Some content that appears in print may not be available in electronic books.

Library of Congress Cataloging-in-Publication Data

Gordon, Virginia N.
  Career advising : an academic advisor's guide / Virginia N.
Gordon.—1st ed.
    p. cm.— (The Jossey-Bass higher and adult education series)
  Includes bibliographical references and index.
  ISBN-13: 978-0-7879-8367-3 (alk. paper)
  ISBN-10: 0-7879-8367-5 (alk. paper)
  1. Counseling in higher education—United States. 2. Vocational
guidance—United States. 3. Career development—United States. 4.
College students—Employment—United States. 5. Faculty advisors—United
States. I. Title. II. Series.
  LB2343.G636 2006
  378.1'9425—dc22

                                                          2005028784

Printed in the United States of America
FIRST EDITION
HB Printing   10 9 8 7 6 5 4 3 2 1

The Jossey-Bass

Higher and Adult Education Series

The National Academic Advising Association

The National Academic Advising Association (NACADA) is the leader within the global higher education community for theory, delivery, application, and advancement of academic advising to enhance student development. Its mission includes

- Affirming the role of academic advising in student success and persistence, thereby supporting institutional mission and vitality.
- Championing the educational role of academic advisors to enhance student learning and development in a diverse world.
- Anticipating and fulfilling the academic advising needs of twenty-first century students, advisors, and institutions.
- Advancing the body of knowledge on academic advising.
- Fostering the talents and contributions of all members and promoting the involvement of diverse populations.

NACADA strives to fulfill this mission through its members by providing resources to enhance student success. These resources include a semiannual professional journal, a quarterly e-publication, regional and national conferences, teleconferences direct to campuses, special publications addressing advising issues, an advisor training video, member commissions to address issues specific to special populations or situations, intensive Institutes, and many other helpful services and resources.

NACADA membership and resource information is available at www.nacada.ksu.edu

Contents

Preface

The necessity for integrating academic and career advising is apparent in today's colleges because of the overwhelming number and scope of academic and career choices that students confront and the complexity of the changing work world they are preparing to enter. Now as never before, academic advisors need to be in tune with the changing workplace and the many factors influencing it. The focus of this book is on advising college students who are in the throes of learning about their academic potential and how their educational choices can lead them to future career-related decisions. Academic advisors are in an ideal position to help students understand the relationships between their academic and career choices and the impact these decisions will have on their future personal and work lives.

Students today are entering a workplace that is unlike any other in U.S. history. Globalization, downsizing, reengineering, and changing organizational structures have left the old workplace unrecognizable. Students entering this new workplace need to be prepared for change and uncertainty. They must acquire the essential knowledge and skills needed to compete in a knowledge-based economy ("Trends," 2003). Academic advisors are well positioned to help students, while they are in college, identify and develop the knowledge and skills that are necessary to succeed in this new economy.

This book is intended for academic advisors and other college personnel who come from a variety of academic disciplines and backgrounds and who wish to learn, expand, or refine their knowledge of career development theory, career information, and career advising practices. Although the title of "academic counselor" is used by some institutions, this book makes a distinction between *career counseling* and *career advising*. The historical paths of these two services have some similarities, but they have many differences in practice. It is not the advisor's role to become a career counselor but to be knowledgeable about how students develop vocationally; to recognize career-related problems; to be a career information expert relative to the academic area they advise; to help students gather and process information; and to be proficient in referring students to career-related resources.

Although many academic advisors provide career information to students in certain circumstances, a much-needed regular application of career-advising methods and techniques is not always practiced. The intent of this book is to identify and describe the knowledge and skills that are required to be effective career advisors. It can serve as a guide through the maze of career information sources that are available in many forms as well as an introduction to other important career-related resources and methods.

Chapter 1 traces the histories of both career counseling and career advising and defines their differences and similarities. The vast array of academic and career services available on most campuses can be either elusive or overwhelming to some students. This chapter describes the various career-related providers on campuses and provides descriptions of their unique roles in serving students. Advisors are encouraged to set career-advising goals based on the academic advising standards provided by the Council for the Advancement of Professional Standards (CAS).

Chapter 2 lists nine advisor competencies required to provide effective career advising. Detailed descriptions of these competencies offer advisors information about areas they might want to expand or refine. The implication for advisor development programs is discussed, with examples provided of activities that might be used for each competency. Chapter 3 presents a career-advising framework that is based on decision-making theory. The *3-I Process* describes three interactive phases—INQUIRE, INFORM, and INTEGRATE—that students pass through as they identify and explore academic and career-related possibilities and make decisions. The first phase of this process, INQUIRE, involves identifying students' academic and career concerns, clarifying their needs, and making appropriate responses. This phase encourages students to ask meaningful questions so that their concerns can be fully understood. It also emphasizes the importance of advisors becoming competent in framing questions in the context of career problem solving. The career concerns that students bring to advisors are described as information deficits, general indecision concerns, and personal concerns related to career decision making. Examples of the career-advising needs of some special student populations are offered as well. The communication skills of listening and questioning are discussed, along with methods for communicating through technology.

Chapter 4 describes the second phase of the 3-I Process, INFORM, which covers the areas of information that are integral to career advising. This phase is concerned with gathering the self-information, educational information, and occupational information that are critical components of career exploration. Many sources of this information are detailed, and the importance of teaching students how to evaluate the information they have collected is discussed. The third phase of the 3-I Process, described in Chapter 5, covers the vital step of helping students INTEGRATE all the knowledge they have accumulated so that a clearer, more concise picture may be composed. Other important aspects of the integrative process, such as the different elements in decision making and some personal factors that influence students' effectiveness in making academic and career decisions, are also discussed. A list of career resources for advisors is offered so that they can be more responsive as they help students integrate the information needed to make realistic, satisfying decisions.

There are many methods and techniques for delivering career information and assistance, and Chapter 6 describes those most common, including group career advising, career courses, computerized career guidance programs, and Internet resources. Different approaches for using these methods in an advising context are described. Finally, Chapter 7 discusses the challenges that advisors and students will face in an ever-changing future. Workplace and higher education trends that are relevant to career advising are described, as are the implications for students and advisors. The competencies that students need to develop while in college in order to succeed in the future workplace and suggestions for how advisors can improve their career-advising practices also are discussed.

Appendix A lists some useful career-advising Web sites that advisors will find helpful as they access information for themselves and for their students. Appendix B offers some case studies of students who are in the throes of career decisions and who represent the three phases of the 3-I Process.

In the beginning of this book, advisors are encouraged to assess their career-advising practices to determine how involved they are in career-related advising activities. They are also encouraged to reflect on these practices and, if they desire, set some personal career-advising goals. At the end of the book, advisors are encouraged to determine whether any of their goals have been met over time. It is hoped that this book will be an incentive for advisors to understand the importance of expanding their career-advising practices and will take some of the mystery out of career-advising resources and approaches.

Columbus, Ohio   Virginia N. Gordon
November 2005

The Author

Virginia N. Gordon is assistant dean emeritus and adjunct associate professor at The Ohio State University. She has extensive experience in teaching, administration, advising, and counseling in higher education settings. Her bibliography includes many books, monographs, book chapters, and articles on advising administration, career counseling, working with undecided students, and advisor training. She is past president of the National Academic Advising Association (NACADA) and the founder and first director of the National Clearinghouse on Academic Advising. Gordon has receive national acclaim and numerous awards for her contributions to the field, the most fitting of which is NACADA's naming its award for outstanding contributions to the field of academic advising the Virginia N. Gordon Award.

1

CAREER COUNSELING AND CAREER ADVISING

Differences and Similarities

When academic advising was initially provided in American colonial colleges, the presidents of the colleges served as counselors and teachers to the male students who matriculated. Later, the faculty took over the role of academic and personal counselor. There was little need for career planning, since the colleges' main role was to prepare young men for the ministry, law, or medicine. During that period there was a clear distinction between a profession and a vocation: clergy, lawyers, and physicians pursued professions; farmers, merchants, and manufacturers pursued vocations (Rudolph, 1962). "The spirit of career preparation was not something new, for in the old-time colleges the student body was composed largely of young men headed for the three learned professions" (p. 341).

In the early part of the nineteenth century, there was great debate about whether colleges should prepare only the professions, that is, law, theology, and medicine, or provide training for "vocational" students as well. This finally came to a head in the Jacksonian Era, when a college education was preferred for some of the expanded career fields, such as journalism, chemistry, art, music, business, and engineering. These new college curricula were considered as important as the ancient courses of study: "All careers demanded an equal hearing and an equal opportunity within the university" (Rudolph, 1962, p. 341).

As the curriculum expanded and became more complex, the need for more individual academic counseling became imperative. As Rudolph (1962) pointed out, the creation of a system of faculty advisors at Johns Hopkins in 1877, "was the first formal recognition that size and the elective curriculum required closer attention to undergraduate guidance than was possible with an increasingly professionally oriented faculty" (p. 460).

Like advising, career counseling has had a long and varied history and has taken shape in many forms (Crites, 1981; Pope, 2000). Although it had been practiced in various contexts before, social reformer Frank Parsons's espousal of the need for "vocational guidance" in his 1909 publication, *Choosing a Vocation*, was the forerunner of today's broader and more complex career counseling practices. The first recorded attempt to use a clinical approach to vocational appraisal was initiated by Morris Viteles, who established a vocational guidance clinic as part of a general psychological clinic in 1920. His psychographic method of job analysis specified the psychological requirements of occupations (Crites, 1981). The famous Hawthorn studies in 1927 made "dramatically clear the importance of human relations, leadership supervision, and worker morale in worker performance and productivity" (Crites, 1981, p. 6). In 1942, Carl Rogers broadened the idea of career counseling as a psychological concept and incorporated his counseling approaches into its theory and practice (Pope, 2000).

Donald Super's *Career Pattern Study*, launched in 1951, was the first long-range research study on career behavior. Super freed career counseling from its static concept of one-time decision making, "drawing attention to the potential contributions of sociology and economics to the field, and placing the study of career behavior in the context of human development" (Crites, 1981, p. 7). Behavioral-oriented career counseling as espoused by Krumboltz (1966) offered new approaches to career decision making, including modeling, goal setting, and reinforcement.

From the psychological tests that were developed during World War I; to the broader research and testing programs initiated during World War II; to the theoretical emphasis in the middle part of the past century; to the theoretically based and more sophisticated approaches that are practiced today, career counseling has emerged as a process and practice that even Frank Parsons might consider amazing.

Although academic advising began in the colonial colleges, the need to assist students with their academic planning became more apparent during the nineteenth century. After the Civil War, many economic and social changes forced individuals to think about their vocations in different ways, and vocational guidance was acceptable. Both academic advising and career counseling made great progress in the twentieth century, especially in the use of theoretical concepts and theories to explain student thought and behavior. National professional organizations emerged to fulfill the need of the two increasingly vital services. Today both provide important, viable resources that meet the needs of a large clientele. The historical paths of academic advising and career counseling, as they have evolved independently of each other, are outlined in Table 1.1.

The Need for an Integrated Approach

The need to integrate academic and career advising is not new. The proliferation of academic disciplines, the complexity of the work world, and the unfailing perception on the part of students that college is preparation for a career, require new thinking about how academic and career advising are intertwined. Academic decisions are never made in isolation; many factors influence students' choices of major, coursework, and ideas about planning for their future careers. Advisors need to be prepared to help students understand how career fields are related to the educational decisions they are making. If advisors don't help their advisees integrate these two areas of information, the students will tap other sources that may not be as accurate, timely, or reliable.

The purpose of this book is to assist academic advisors and other professional personnel who come from a variety of academic disci-

Table 1.1 Historical Perspectives

Academic Advising	Career Counseling
Academic advising was first performed by college presidents in colonial colleges; later by their faculty.	Need for vocational guidance was recognized because of economic and social conditions after the Civil War (for example, industrialization, immigration, child labor).
Expansion of college curricula and the introduction of electives in the nineteenth century created a need for more individual academic counseling.	First vocational guidance clinic established in 1920s at University of Pennsylvania, where vocational appraisal was used for psychological requirements of occupations.
William Rainey Harper, University of Chicago president, in 1905 suggested there needed to be a "scientific study of the student himself."	Frank Parsons's espousal of more extensive vocational guidance in early 1900s started a more comprehensive vocational guidance movement.
After WWI, feelings and attitudes of students in addition to aptitudes were taken into account by advisors.	WWI's need to screen draftees for assignment to jobs in military spawned an era of testing development.
By 1930, most colleges had formal faculty advising programs; college/department advising centers were established during the next decades.	First edition of the Dictionary of Occupational Titles (DOT), which defined more than 18,000 U.S. occupations, was published by the U.S. Employment Service in 1939.
Theoretical concepts were incorporated into advising frameworks in 1970s and 1980s; student development theory began influencing advising practice.	Psychological, sociological, and economic theories of career continued to emerge in the 1940s to 1960s (for example, Super, Tiedeman, Holland); today old theories are being revised and new ones are emerging.
The National Academic Advising Association was formed in 1979 to fill a need for the growing professionalism of academic advising; in 2006 the association had about 9,000 members.	The National Vocational Guidance Association celebrated its ninetieth anniversary in 2004; many other career-related professional organizations have evolved.
Academic advising today is recognized as a critical service; the need for academic and career advising is reflected in a complex, ever-changing world.	Career counseling today encompasses a complex set of factors and needs that are met with diverse types of resources and techniques.

plines and who have little formal knowledge about career theory, career information, or career counseling. It is intended to provide a guide to the career-advising information and skills needed by advisors to help students better understand how their college experiences can prepare them for an increasingly complex workplace. Many advisors have long recognized how students consciously or unconsciously equate their academic major decisions with future career possibilities. The need to integrate academic and career information is critical in helping students with the curricular and extracurricular choices they are continually making.

Student Career-Advising Needs

All students need career advising, even those who enter college already decided on an academic major. Some very decided students may have based their choices on realistic information about their personal abilities and talents to succeed in the academic rigors of their discipline. They still may need assistance, however, with researching the connections between their academic choices and the related complex array of career possibilities. Other students choose an academic major based on very little information about what the curriculum entails and how their own strengths and limitations might predict satisfaction and success. Still others enter college admittedly undecided about a major or the possible career fields related to them (Gordon & Sears, 2004; Steele, 2003). The last two groups of students, in particular, need to be involved in exploring many possibilities and require the coordinated efforts of academic advisors and other campus career services.

The initial and primary contact that most college students have as they begin their college experience is their assigned academic advisors. What students bring to the advising relationship will depend on their maturity, their academic goals (or lack of goals), and where they are in the academic and career decision-making processes. Some are not concerned about a career direction at this time, while others have chosen a major because it leads to a specific career field.

As indicated, certain kinds of students need more concentrated help with career exploration and decision making. Undecided students require a more focused approach, since they need to be actively engaged in an exploratory mode (Gordon, 1995; Schein & Laff, 1997). A critical aspect of this exploratory process is to consider the career implications of the academic alternatives students are considering. Exploratory students need to engage in an organized search through which they collect, evaluate, and apply career as well as academic information to their personal interests and abilities. Understanding the career decision-making process and learning the skills required for making decisions will be useful throughout a student's life.

This same concentrated approach needs to be applied by students who are in the process of changing majors. Some students are denied entrance into their first choice of major because of selective or competitive admissions policies. Others find the coursework in their initial choice of major is not as interesting as they thought it would be, while others learn that they do not have the academic backgrounds to succeed in the major. There are many other reasons why students change majors, but regardless of the cause, they need special assistance to explore academic and career alternatives.

Older adult students make up a large part of the college student population today. Some may be starting second careers, while others are in school to improve their chances of entering more challenging and better-paying work. Although older students may have more career experience than traditional-age students, they often need academic and career advising that takes into account their unique family and economic situations.

Many other special populations, such as students from different racial or ethnic backgrounds, require advisors to be sensitive to the circumstances that influence their individual academic and career choices. Family and cultural influences can have a positive or negative impact on the way students engage in the academic and career planning and decision-making processes. Advisors must be aware of the role that cultural differences play in influencing career exploration behavior.

All college students, regardless of their academic direction or degree of decidedness, need specific information about the career possibilities in their fields, information about how to mount a job search, an awareness of the dramatic changes occurring in the workplace, and the skills needed to be marketable (Kummerow, 2000). All students need career advising that is geared to their educational level and developmental needs (Kramer, 2000). This means that advisors must focus on each student's unique place in the academic, career, and life-planning process.

Academic advisors, regardless of their past training or in what setting they perform their advising duties, need to have a solid base of knowledge about how students approach the academic and career decision-making processes. They also need to acquire the advising skills associated with helping students explore, evaluate, and integrate the academic and career information that is so critical to career and life planning.

The focus of this book is primarily on advising college students who are in the throes of learning about their academic potential and how their educational choices might lead to their place in the work world. In order to be on the leading edge of teaching and advising students in the twenty-first century, faculty and nonteaching advisors must be open to new insights and knowledge about changing student populations. They must adapt their advising and teaching techniques to help prepare students to live and assume leadership in a very different world from the one in which the advisors grew up. This includes expanding their expertise for helping students with the transition from college to the workplace. Through the academic/career-advising relationship, students can be empowered to plan strategically for their futures.

Career Counseling and Career Advising Defined

Although the title of "academic counselor" is used by some institutions, this book makes a distinction between *counseling* and *advising*. Some professional advisors have counseling backgrounds, and their advising approaches may be framed by a counseling perspective. Because of their counselor training, they also may be more knowledgeable about career development and planning. The vast majority of faculty and full-time advisors, however, do not have (nor do they need) that background. An advisor job satisfaction survey sponsored by the National Academic Advising Association (NACADA) (Donnelly, 2005), found that 74 percent of the nearly 1,700 advisor respondents did not have a counseling degree.

Academic advisors are not expected to be career counselors but to assist students in gathering and processing the information needed to engage in realistic *academically related* career planning. As they work with individual students, advisors need the skills to determine whether they have the competencies to assist with career-related problems or whether they need to refer students to more focused and appropriate resources. Although the two terms, *advising* and *counseling,* signify two different approaches, there are similarities in the expertise required for each. If any confusion about their practice exists, it can be cleared up by understanding the differences and similarities of the two.

Reardon and Lumsden (2003) make the distinction between *career services* and *career-planning services.* "Career services include career planning and development interventions, cooperative education and experiential career education programs, and job placement and employment services. Career planning services, in contrast, are concentrated in the areas of career development (not placement), counseling, advising, assessment, information and decision making interventions" (p. 167). Descriptions of some of the career-planning services that are offered follow.

Career Counseling

When discussing career counseling, certain terms are used interchangeably, although they have different meanings. The term *vocation* is not used very often today; *career* is a more definitive term for reflecting the current approach, which encompasses a constellation of work, family, and leisure roles played over a lifetime. In 1981, Crites defined *career counseling* as "an interpersonal process focused upon assisting an individual to make an appropriate career decision" (p. 11). A more recent definition describes how the career counseling function has broadened. Career counseling assists students to "self-reflect, restructure beliefs, mature and deepen their personalities, and answer the question 'Who am I?'" (Hartung & Niles, 2000, p. 4). The American Counseling Association (ACA) (2005) describes the responsibilities of college counselors as: (1) resolving emotional and other problems that interfere with academic success, (2) designing an academic program that meets students' personal needs and career objectives, (3) identifying sources of financial aid, and (4) securing employment after graduation (p. 2).

A newer term that is being used today is *career coaching*. Career coaches come from a variety of backgrounds. Some are professional career counselors, while others have gleaned their expertise from working in business and other related areas. Career coaches provide guidance and support for individuals who are already in the workforce but who wish to make changes. They use various tools and coaching techniques to help with career planning, advancement, and management. They help clients identify their skills, make better career choices, and help them become more productive and valuable workers (Chung & Gfroerer, 2003). Some of the career-planning techniques and methods used in coaching, such as skill development and information collection, are adaptable to counseling college students as well.

Academic Advising

Definitions of *academic advising*, like career counseling, have broadened over the years. In 1979, Grites described the state of academic advising at that time as "a function in which faculty and students consulted about the student's selection of major and courses and proceeded through the scheduling process" (p. 8). One classic advising model is proposed by O'Banion (1972), who defines academic advising as a process that helps students develop their full potential. He describes five dimensions of the process: (1) exploration of life goals, (2) exploration of vocational goals, (3) program choice, (4) course choice, and (5) scheduling courses. He emphasized that exploring life and vocational goals must be accomplished before the selection of a major and coursework can be made effectively. In retrospect, O'Banion (1994) indicates that if revising his model today, he would "review the impact and potential of technology" on it (p. 119). He also reemphasizes the need to identify the skills, knowledge, and attitudes required of academic advisors for completing the five steps in the advising process that he outlined previously.

Crookston (1972) was the first to use the term *developmental advising*, and since then there have been many reactions to its merit and to its applications to advising practice. Crookston proposed that developmental advising incorporates a relationship in which there is an agreement between advisor and advisee that responsibilities are shared. He defined developmental advising as a systematic process through which students set and achieve their academic, personal, and career goals with the support of their academic advisors and the institution's resources. As an opposing advising style, he described a more prescriptive approach in which advisors take the initiative to make decisions for the students. Creamer and Creamer (1994) have defined the many themes in the developmental advising literature and encourage its practice. Pardee (1994), on the other hand, points out the "complex web of constraints that conspire against developmental advising" (p. 59), which includes student behavior, advisors' skills and motivation, and institutional factors such as enrollment levels and delivery systems. In spite of that, academic advising is recognized today as more learning centered than prescriptive; more all-encompassing than narrow. Today, the process views students through a developmental lens that identifies their aspirations, interests, and abilities and integrates these personal characteristics into academic, career, and life planning.

The concept of academic advising is described in a statement from the National Academic Advising Association (NACADA) (2004). The goals of academic advising as stated in its preamble are to "teach students to understand the meaning of higher education, teach students to understand the purpose of the curriculum, and to foster students' intellectual and personal development toward academic success and lifelong learning" (p. 1).

Through the academic advising process, students learn to take responsibility for setting goals as well as planning the steps to implement them. It recognizes that the choice of major is not necessarily an isolated decision but merely one facet in preparing for a career that may have an impact on the type of work students enter and the lifestyle they wish to achieve.

Butler (1995) suggests that academic advisors and career counselors use some of the same techniques and focus on similar student concerns. He contends, however, that advisors "are more concerned with helping students learn information-seeking, analytical, and decision-making skills so they can meet the institutional expectations for successful academic achievement, graduation, and employment" (p. 108).

Career Advising

Career advising may be thought of as a less psychologically intensive approach than career counseling. The emphasis is on information and helping students understand the relationships between their educational choices and general career fields rather than how to cope with intense career-related personal concerns. Career advising helps students understand how their personal interests, abilities, and values might predict success in the academic and career fields they are considering and how to form their academic and career goals accordingly. Table 1.2 summarizes some of the differences between *career counseling* and *career advising*.

Some advisors do not engage in career advising because they feel they lack the background and training or because they don't view it as their responsibility. This may put some students at a disadvantage, however, if the students don't receive the academic and occupational information that is critical for informed, timely decisions. The view of career advising as an integral, natural part of academic advising is used in the pages that follow. Perhaps some day the term *career advising* will disappear when it becomes so ingrained in the academic advising process that its separate designation will no longer be necessary.

Who Does It?

A better understanding of career advising and career counseling can be achieved by examining the campus professionals who engage in academic and career counseling activities and the context in which they work.

Academic Advisors. As in the past, faculty members still comprise the majority of academic advisors (Habley, 2004). Faculty advisors usually are assigned students who are majoring in their academic disciplines. A growing number of institutions use full-time professional staff in addition to faculty. Professional advisors come from many academic disciplines and backgrounds. Professional advisors work in a variety of settings, such as advising centers, academic departments, or living-learning residence hall programs. Some advising center staffs are comprised of both faculty and professional advisors.

Table 1.2   A Comparison of Career Advising and Career Counseling

	Career Advising	Career Counseling
Purpose	To help students make academic decisions that incorporate knowledge of academic/career relationships and possibilities	To assist students with career development problems; may be therapeutic
Content	Integration of self, academic, and career information leading to academic decision making	Resolution of career-related problems and concerns
Methods and Techniques	Individual/group advising Academic coursework Internet searches Computer-assisted programs Workshops Distance	Individual/group counseling Testing expertise Personal and career information resources as needed
Advisor/Counselor Competencies	Advising skills (for example, teaching, communication) Knowledge of career decision-making theoretical frameworks Technological competence	Job-search related assistance if indicated Counseling skills and techniques Assessment knowledge and skills Knowledge of career decision-making theory Technological competence
Outcomes	Realistic and satisfying academic decisions made Knowledge of related career fields known Plans for implementing decisions carried out Decision-making skills learned	Career development problems resolved Knowledge and skills for future career/life planning acquired

Career Counselors. College career counselors also work in a variety of settings. They may be found in counseling services, career planning and/or placement centers, or in centers where academic advising and career counseling are integrated. They provide the more traditional career counseling functions, such as helping students with career self-assessment, job search and job placement activities, or counseling students who are experiencing more stressful situations such as coping with academic and career transitions and indecisiveness.

Student Personnel Workers. Some student personnel professionals elect to work as academic or career counselors in any of the settings described. They often are found in community college advising and career centers. Their training may have involved graduate-level coursework in career-related subjects or work experiences in higher education.

Placement Counselors. Some colleges establish job placement centers where the primary function is to assist students in the job-search process. Many centers combine career-planning activities with the placement function. Placement professionals come from many backgrounds including those with business experience.

Another important career resource on many campuses is the *career library.* These repositories of career information are often coordinated by professional librarians, but are sometimes part of a career center where paraprofessionals may have day-to-day responsibilities. Career librarians can assist students in their search for career information in many formats, including printed materials, computer-assisted programs, and the Internet.

Career Services Interaction

As can be seen from the descriptions given, there is great overlap in the way and from whom students receive academic and career information and assistance. Every campus has its particular way of presenting these important services. McCalla-Wriggins (2000) points out that collaboration between academic advising and career resources can occur both formally and informally. Many advisors form their own networks of colleagues throughout their campus and direct students to them when specific needs are evident. Joint meetings between academic and career-planning staffs can be most effective in initiating and coordinating activities between the two services. Advisory boards and steering committees are examples of more formal bodies through which collaboration between advising and career services is managed.

Academic advisors need to know what each of the career-related services on their campus offers so that referrals can be targeted to students' particular needs. Some students may need referral to counseling services, for example, when they are having difficulty coping with family pressures to choose a major or career field that the student doesn't want or cannot attain. Placement offices can provide students with information about where former students with certain majors found jobs upon graduation. Other resources that advisors must be knowledgeable about in order to make effective referrals are career courses, internships, career libraries, academic departments, or career fairs and other career-related campus events.

The intent of this book is to identify the knowledge and skills that are required to be effective career advisors in this new age and to act as a resource guide for the information and techniques that are basic for helping students become more astute and knowledgeable lifelong decision makers.

Career-Advising Principles

There are certain basic tenets that are at the core of career advising. A few examples follow:

- Choosing and maintaining a career is a lifelong process. College is only one decision point in a long series of career choices and transitions.

- The career decision-making process itself incorporates knowledge of one's self, information about educational opportunities, and facts about the work world. Integrating these areas of information in an organized way can help students identify realistic academic and occupational alternatives.
- Career decisions are value based. Clarifying a personally valid set of beliefs and acting upon them is critical to a satisfying career.
- Effective career decision-making skills are used over a lifetime and can be learned.
- There are no right or wrong decisions, only satisfying and unsatisfying ones. Future events may affect a good decision in ways unforeseen at the time it was made.
- Sex, race, or age should never be a barrier to exploring any and all possible career options.

The most effective academic advisors develop and continually refine their knowledge of the concepts and practical applications of career exploration, choice, and planning.

Setting Integrative Career-Advising Goals

Based on these and other principles that advisors construct from their own experiences and values, it is important for them to set goals for their advising so that they can measure their skill levels and effectiveness with students over time. Among many types of evaluation, self-evaluation is a recognized method for helping advisors determine in what areas their performance levels are high and what areas need to improve. In ACT, Inc.'s sixth national survey, *The Status of Academic Advising* (2004), 86 percent of reporting institutions indicated they used self-evaluation to formally evaluate advisor performance. In the ACT survey, some of the goals that are listed for advising programs are applicable to self-evaluation as well:

- Assisting students in self-understanding and self-acceptance (values clarification; understanding abilities, interests, and limitations)

- Assisting students in considering life goals by relating interests, skills, abilities, and values to careers, the world of work, and the nature and purpose of higher education

- Assisting students in developing an educational plan consistent with life goals and objectives

- Assisting students in developing decision-making skills

- Referring students to other institutional or community support services

- Assisting students in evaluating or reevaluating progress toward established goals and educational plans

Examining their advising practices against these goals is an excellent way for advisors to evaluate what areas they regularly incorporate in their advising sessions and what areas they do not.

Another vehicle for setting career goals is to use those outlined in the Council for the Advancement of Professional Standards (CAS) guidelines (Miller, 1997). CAS sets standards for the important elements within an effective advising program, such as mission, program, leadership, organization, and management. It specifies that academic advising programs "must identify relevant and desirable student learning and development outcomes" (Council for the Advancement of Professional Standards for Higher Education [CAS], 2005, p. 1). One of the learning domains included in these learning outcomes is "career choices" (p. 2). The achievement indicators for this domain are that a successful student can:

- Articulate career choices based on assessment of interests, values, skills, and abilities

- Document knowledge, skills, and accomplishments resulting from formal education, work experience, community service, and volunteer experiences

- Make the connections between classroom and out-of-class learning
- Construct a résumé with clear job objectives and evidence of related knowledge, skills, and accomplishments
- Articulate the characteristics of a preferred work environment
- Comprehend the world of work
- Take steps to initiate a job search or seek advanced education

Another domain identified by the CAS standards relevant to career advising is the importance of "clarified values." This learning outcome states that a student must be able to "identify personal, work and lifestyle values and explain how they influence decision making" (CAS, 2005, p. 1).

These student learning and development outcomes as defined by CAS endorse the necessity for career advising and can be used as a guide for advisors as they work to refine and rethink this important part of their advising expertise. Checklist 1.3 offers career-related questions suggested by the CAS standards that advisors can use to evaluate the dimensions of their career advising. Implicit in these CAS learning domains are the knowledge and skills advisors need in order to assist students in overcoming educational and personal problems and skill deficiencies.

These guidelines can act as a stimulus for considering the goals advisors want to set for themselves. Although some advising centers or departments have developed evaluation forms, advisors need to generate their own lists of personal advising goals, including those pertaining to career information and advice. There are specific areas of expertise in the career domain that some advisors may need to expand or refine. In addition to the goals mentioned, examples of more practical career-related outcomes goals are offered following. Advisors should consider:

- Establishing personal career-advising principles and goals by which they will advise

Checklist 1.3   Career-Advising Questions

As an academic advisor I am now discussing with students:

___ The characteristics of the work environment they prefer at this point and why these characteristics are appealing to them

___ Possible career fields based on students' interests as expressed through choice of major or through other strong areas of interest

___ Possible career fields based on students' work values or what students say is important in their work lives

___ Possible career fields in which students' strongest abilities and skills would be used to their fullest advantage

___ How to identify students' knowledge, skills, and accomplishments from their formal education, work experience, community service, and volunteer experiences

___ Where and how students can acquire this essential knowledge and develop these skills if they do not have enough relevant experiences

___ How what they are learning in the classroom can be used in future work tasks, habits, and attitudes as well in life tasks

___ How the world of work is continually changing and how students can develop the skills needed to successfully enter and thrive in a variety of work environments

___ The importance of acquiring while in college technological skills essential to students' future employment

___ How students can begin to plan the steps they will need to take to search for a job after graduation, or the steps needed to plan for advanced education

___ How students can document the knowledge, skills, and accomplishments they have already acquired in a résumé format and what they can do to strengthen their general marketability

Source: Based on the "career choices" domain of the CAS standards (CAS, 2005).

- Developing and categorizing a list of career concerns that students bring to them so they can identify those they are prepared to help and those they need to refer
- Expanding their knowledge and understanding of career and student development theories

- Studying career decision-making styles and strategies that both their students and they use so they are more sensitive to the dynamics that are in play
- Knowing firsthand the career resources on their campuses, including individual and group career counseling services, career courses, career libraries, and job search and placement services
- Bookmarking career-related Internet sites that they use frequently with students in their offices
- Developing a career-advising library for their offices that includes career-specific resources relevant to the academic areas they advise
- Creating career-related handouts applicable to the majors they advise
- Improving their referral skills so that they are more focused on specific career-related needs
- Becoming familiar with the type of career tests and assessments and the computerized career guidance systems available at their career counseling centers so they can refer more effectively
- Taking part in advisor development programs that can expand their career-advising expertise

Setting career-advising goals can help advisors focus on the career-related assistance they are equipped to offer and help to identify the areas they still need to improve. Research indicates that advisors' stated philosophies or goals for advising are consistent with the behaviors they display during their advising contacts (Daller, Creamer, & Creamer, 1997). Consciously thinking about and committing to paper the career-advising goals advisors want to accomplish will increase their confidence and ability to advise in the career domain.

Identifying and Assessing
Career-Advising Outcomes

Making a list of career-advising goals is not useful unless advisors periodically measure the impact they have on changing students' behavior. Although Banta, Hansen, Black, and Jackson (2002) advise using outcome assessments for examining the overall quality of advising, these are also valuable tools for measuring the effect an advisor has on students' career exploration and decision-making activities. Abelman and Molina (2001) used "intrusive advising" with academically at-risk students and found it was an effective method for improving student performance. They defined *intrusive advising* as having personal contact, generating student responsibility for decision making, assisting in resolving causes of poor performance, and negotiating agreements for future actions. They suggest that intrusive advising is invasive because it is personal rather than merely professional. This is an example of how one advising approach can suggest certain desirable advising outcomes. Intrusiveness can generate personal contact between student and advisor, encourage student responsibility for problem solving and decision making, and encourage planning for future actions (Grites & Gordon, 2000). Intrusive career advising should result in students' acquisition of career knowledge (from information gathering), their ability to process the information in a personal context, and their taking a variety of actions to use it (for example, schedule coursework that teaches marketable skills, sign up for an internship program, use the Internet to job hunt). When intrusive advising is practiced in career advising, it can be effective in moving students to action, which is a desirable advising outcome.

Assessing the goals advisors set for themselves may require follow-up phone calls, e-mail surveys, questions asked of career planning offices, focus groups, departmental questionnaires, or other methods compatible with the advisors' goals and advising situation. Setting goals and measuring outcomes are critical parts of any advising endeavor, and it is important in career advising as well. Advisors need to follow up with students to determine if their career-advising methods are working and to use the feedback to improve and expand their advising in this area when indicated.

Summary

Both academic advising and career counseling have long and fascinating histories. Each makes an important contribution to students' success and satisfaction. It is important, however, to make the distinction between career counseling and career advising. Academic advisors are not expected to be career counselors, but as career advisors they can assist students in gathering information and providing advice that leads to informed and realistic academically related career planning.

There are many differences and similarities between career counseling and career advising. These include the different levels and methods for disseminating career information, the emphasis placed on academic relationships to career fields, and how academic interests, academic abilities, and values might predict success in the academic and related career fields they are considering.

Many different kinds of professionals on campus are engaged in providing career information, assessment, advising, counseling, and placement. Cooperation between academic advising and career services is critical if these functions are to assist students effectively.

Career-advising principles are offered that can guide advisors' application to involving students in career exploration, choice, and planning. Advisors need to establish career-advising goals so that they can determine the career-related knowledge and skills they already possess and the advising outcomes they want to accomplish. In order to do this, they need to develop the competencies ascribed to becoming effective career advisors. These competencies are described in the next chapter.

2

CAREER-ADVISING COMPETENCIES

Career advising does not require advisor competencies that are not already known and practiced by academic advisors. Basic advising skills such as communication, teaching, and referral are no different from those used in regular student advising contacts. When integrating career-related knowledge and skills in academic advising, however, certain advisor competencies are emphasized. Expanded areas of career knowledge might be required to effectively offer students specific types of career information and advice. Theoretical frameworks, for example, provide insights into how students change their perceptions of the meaning of career over time. Technological and assessment competencies may need to be adapted to more specialized uses. Some of the competencies that advisors need to review or expand when giving career advice are described in the following sections.

Advisor Competencies

Theoretical Competency

Understanding theoretical frameworks can provide insights and give direction and meaning to advisors' daily contacts with students. Although there are many theories with which advisors can shape their work, several attempt to explain how college students develop career-wise. Much has been written about developmental advising and its importance in shaping a student-centered advising system. Although advisors' primary contacts with students involve academic information and concerns, a developmental advisor understands that students exhibit a wide array of career-related interests and degrees of maturity.

Relevant Theoretical Frameworks. One way advisors can understand students' perceptions and behaviors in regard to academic and career exploration and decision making is to acquire a basic knowledge of who college students are, how they change during the college years, and how they develop an academic and career identity.

It is not the intention of this book to offer in detail the many useful theories about how students grow personally and vocationally or how their beliefs and values influence their thoughts and behaviors. The brief descriptions that follow provide a general introduction to some important theoretical frameworks that advisors who are not familiar with student and career development theories might pursue in more depth on their own. Excellent summaries of these theories can be found in many other sources (for example, Brown, 2002; Evans, Forney, & Guido-DiBrito, 1998; Niles & Harris-Bowlsbey, 2002; Savickas & Walsh, 1996; Zunker, 2001). Those that follow offer insights into how individuals are involved in career development, particularly during the college years.

Life-Span Theory. Donald Super (1990) indicates that career development is a continuous, lifelong process. College students are making career decisions during what Super terms the "exploration stage," when they become aware of the need to plan for the future. During this period, students collect information about themselves and occupations and explore the degree to which these occupations enable them to implement their self-concepts. During this time, they are clarifying their values, skills, and interests and making connections to some initial choices based on these attributes. They eventually take action to implement their educational and career decisions based on the occupational preferences they have specified.

Super also offers the useful concept of *career maturity*, or students' readiness to tackle the demands that face them. Many advisors have encountered students who don't seem to be motivated to take any steps toward making or implementing academic or career decisions. According to Super's concept, these students have not completed the career development tasks necessary to cope with the decision-making process at this particular time. They are not as mature as their chronological age suggests, or when the institution's policies and rules say they should be.

When applying some of Super's ideas to career advising, advisors can use them to understand that students are in various stages of developing their "life plans." Advisors can help students through the academic and career exploration and decision-making processes by raising students' awareness of the need to plan and who, how, and where on campus they can find assistance to support them through this process.

Person-Environment Theory. John Holland's (1997) theory of vocational types and person-environment interactions is one of the most useful in helping students make connections between the "Who am I?" question and possible majors and occupations. Holland characterizes people by their resemblance to six personality types: Realistic, Investigative, Artistic, Social, Enterprising, and Conventional. Each personality type is the product of how the individual interacts with a variety of personal and cultural forces. Each type has different interests, competencies, and dispositions. Each of the six work environments (given the same names) also has distinct features, and certain types of people are drawn to those environments that are congruent with their personal characteristics. Holland states that when individuals select occupations that are congruent with their personality types, they will be satisfied with their work. When they are in occupations that are incongruent with their personalities, they are not as happy or satisfied.

Perhaps no other theory has been adapted to college career resources as has Holland's. One of the instruments measuring his person-environment interaction concepts, the Self-Directed Search (SDS), is widely used in print form, through the Internet, and in computer-assisted programs. Some campus career libraries have arranged their resources (including their majors) by Holland's "codes." The *Dictionary of Holland Occupational Codes* (3rd edition)

(Gottfredson & Holland, 1996) provides a list of more than 12,000 occupations by Holland codes. Once students have determined their Holland "type of personality," they can connect it directly to a wide array of occupations and majors. This helps them confirm a choice or identify alternatives that they can explore in more depth. More practical Holland applications in career advising are suggested in Chapters 5 and 6.

Learning Theory. John Krumboltz (1996) calls his theory the "social learning theory of career decision making" (p. 60). It describes how many learning experiences combine to shape the individual's career path. People are exposed to many learning opportunities as a result of their social, cultural, economic, geographic, and political circumstances. Thus people are exposed to learning experiences that are unique to them. Krumboltz acknowledges the role of genetic endowments that are inherited qualities as well as environmental conditions and events that are out of the person's control. Career decision making is influenced by an assessment of ourselves (that is, our interests and values) and the conclusions we draw about ourselves when comparing our performances with others. A student who has positive experiences in certain subjects, such as math and science, for example, will be apt to want to learn more about these subjects. On the other hand, students who have negative experiences in math will try to avoid it.

The acquisition of "task approach skills" is another important concept in career decision making. Students need to clarify their interests, values, and skills, gather occupational information, and integrate this into decision making. Task approach skills include "work habits, mental set, emotional responses, cognitive processes, and problem-solving skills" (Krumboltz, 1996, p. 60).

The goal of career advising, therefore, is to facilitate the acquisition of academic and career skills and habits, and explore interests and other personal qualities within the learning environment. Using Krumboltz's concepts, advisors can be seen as "coaches, educators, and mentors." Advisors can help students become more aware of what they need to learn in order to make career decisions and to be adaptable in an ever-changing environment.

Cognitive Information Processing. Peterson, Sampson, and Reardon (1991) have offered a newer way of thinking about career development through "cognitive information processing (CIP)." They theorize that career choice is a problem-solving activity. Their approach emphasizes the cognitive aspect of decision making. They indicate that career choices are based on how we think and feel. "The quality of our career depends on how well we learn to make career decisions and solve career problems" (Reardon, Lenz, Sampson, & Peterson, 2000, p. 16). The authors use a sequential procedure known as CASVE that can improve the way career problem solving is approached. The CASVE cycle includes the processing skills of communication, analysis, synthesis, valuing, and execution.

Information processing focuses on how to locate, store, and use information in the decision-making process. An information-processing pyramid is used to demonstrate the components of career decision making. The bottom of the pyramid contains the knowledge domain that includes knowledge of self and occupations. The second level includes knowing how decisions are made. The top of the pyramid involves the individual's order of thinking while the decision-making process is taking place ("executive processing"). For example, some students choose a major before they focus on exploring occupations, while others may focus on their preferred lifestyle before working on an occupational choice. The goal of this approach is to help individuals improve the quality of their thinking (metacognitions) in the executive processing domain, or the top of the pyramid.

Information processing is a useful concept in helping students who are struggling with major and career decisions. Not only do students need information, but they must understand how they organize their thinking during the decision-making process, in particular. They need to be aware of metacognitions or thoughts, especially negative thoughts that "short circuit" the problem-solving process and how to increase positive metacognitive thoughts. Changing negative thoughts to positive ones, according to Peterson et al. (1991), is essential to good decision making but may require persistence, motivation, and outside assistance. Sampson, Reardon, Peterson, and Lenz (2003) suggest ways that practitioners can learn to deliver career resources and services through the CIP approach to career problem solving and decision making.

Mayhall and Burg (2002) used the cognitive information-processing pyramid in a solution-focused advising approach with undecided students. The self-knowledge and occupational knowledge domains are at its base; the second level contains the decision-making domain; and the top of the pyramid is the domain where actions are evaluated. "By encouraging students to explore past experiences in which they felt accomplishment, advisors use solution-focused based therapy to assist students in evaluating interests, identifying strengths in character, and discovering abilities" (p. 77).

Values-Based Approach. It has long been recognized that what one values or thinks important plays a vital role in academic and career decision making. The values-based model of Duane Brown (1995) emphasizes that personal and work values can help to explain and guide behavior. Values are core beliefs that individuals use to evaluate their own behavior and that of others. Students need to identify, clarify, and prioritize their values if they are to make satisfying career decisions. For a job to be satisfying, for example, it must allow individuals to engage in work tasks that they consider important and worthwhile. When a person's values are in conflict with their school or work situation, they are more likely to be dissatisfied. Values are also the foundation for goal setting.

Values are such a critical aspect of career decision making that advisors must be sensitive to the values students are expressing in their ideas about major and occupational choices. For example, if a student is indicating a strong interest in pursuing a social work major but expresses the need for a job that pays a high salary, the advisor might point out the conflict of this major choice with the expressed value. Values are developed through family, school, church, media, culture, and other significant influences. Advisors must be aware of possible generational differences in the way values and beliefs are acquired and expressed. Baby Boomers' perception of the importance that work plays in one's lifestyle, for example, may be different from those who belong to Generation X.

Student Development Theories. One of the most widely used theories to explain how college students grow and change is that of Arthur Chickering (Chickering & Reisser, 1993). Chickering indicates that traditional-age students develop in an orderly way, accomplishing certain developmental tasks as they move through their college years. He describes seven developmental tasks or vectors that they need to accomplish during this period of their lives. These tasks include: (1) developing competence, (2) managing emotions, (3) moving through autonomy toward interdependence, (4) developing mature interpersonal relationships, (5) establishing identity, (6) developing purpose, and (7) developing integrity. A vector, according to Chickering, is a developmental task that has specific content, shows up at certain times in life, and takes two to seven years to resolve. Although these tasks occur in order, students may be dealing with several at one time. Older students may be recycling a vector that they had accomplished earlier in life.

The vector that involves career is *developing purpose*. The tasks involved in this vector are in three areas: education, career plans, and planning a mature lifestyle. Examples of tasks that involve educational plans are to set educational goals and to see the relationship between study and other aspects of life. Examples of career planning are to develop an awareness of the world of work and where one's interests and strengths might fit, to synthesize knowledge of self and the work world, and to begin to implement a vocational decision. The tasks involved in developing mature lifestyle plans include developing a future orientation that balances vocational aspirations and future family plans, an attitude of tentative commitment to future plans, and a sense of direction to identify the next steps in life.

Working through these seven vectors is crucial to the college student's passage into adulthood. Chickering's ideas are useful to advisors, because knowing that students display common developmental issues and concerns promotes an understanding of many of their thoughts and behaviors. As students develop career purposes, advisors can assist them in becoming more aware of what is involved in educational and career planning and decision making. Advisors can help students become more aware of what academic, career, and life planning involves, that compromises must be made, encourage them to set short- and long-term goals, and help them understand that clarifying values is a vital part of the decision-making process.

Another theory that is useful to advisors is William Perry's scheme of intellectual and ethical development (1999). Perry's ideas help us understand how students approach thinking and learning. Perry describes how students move from a closed view of what they are learning to an openness and broadening of how they assimilate knowledge. As they are capable of more complex reasoning, they are able to challenge and be challenged by new ideas and ways of thinking. Students need to understand the difference between information and knowledge. Intellectual development requires a larger degree of personal interaction with the educational environment, and advisors are in a perfect position to encourage and foster this development.

The Perry model is comprised of nine positions or stages, each representing a qualitatively different mode of thinking about the nature of knowledge. The nine positions may be grouped into three more abstract categories of dualism, relativism, and commitment with relativism. Dualistic students who see things as black or white, right or wrong, need to be *challenged* to the next level (multiplicity) by large amounts of experiential learning and a high degree of diversity (for example, through the curriculum, assessment, field trips, occupational interviewing). They also need *support* through a high level of structure and a personal atmosphere (for example, structured syllabi, specific instructions, individual feedback).

According to Perry, students move from a closed perspective of decision making and accompanying responsibility to a more open and pluralistic view of alternatives (Gordon, 1981). It is helpful to advisors to understand the different lenses through which their students see their world. Students' perceptions of teachers' or advisors' roles and their own role as learner are colored by these lenses. Perry's ideas help advisors understand that different levels of advice are needed as students grow in the way they approach knowledge and learning.

The theoretical concepts mentioned are only a few of the possible frameworks that advisors might use in developing their own philosophy of advising and how they want to interact with students. Exploring these theories in more depth will expand advisors' understanding of students in general and individual students in particular. Acquiring theoretical competence is a critical but sometimes neglected component of advisor training programs.

Decision-Making Competency

If you ask students *how* they make decisions, they might have difficulty answering because it is often difficult to separate decisions from the decision-making process. Career decisions, like all others, must be made by the student, but advisors can help them become more aware of the decision-making process and how students personally approach this important life task. Advisors can help students ask the right questions, find the necessary information, help them put the information into perspective, and assist them with taking the steps necessary to complete the process.

There are many complex factors in career decision making, and advisors are only exposed to one millisecond in a lifetime of decisions that students will make. Some areas that might help advisors expand their decision-making competencies are the following:

Stating the Problem Succinctly. Since the advisor-advisee relationship is usually short term, defining the concern that the student expresses in precise, clear language is a critical step. Advisors can help to screen out questions or expressed concerns that are unrelated to the immediate problem. What information is the student working with? Is it relevant to the immediate problem, or should it be used later in the process? Advisors may hear students express problems that have many facets, and the advisors' role is to help separate those that are not part of the immediate concern. For example, a business student who received a D in a required math course may be scheduling the next sequential course. He is making excuses for not doing well in the first course, but is giving assurances that he can handle the second one in spite of it. The advisor can explain the ramifications of the student's decision by pointing out that he is not building the essential math foundation for his curriculum.

Collecting and Using Information. As outlined in Chapter 3, there is a need to gather information that is directly connected to the problem at hand. Some students collect and analyze information in an imprecise way. There is a tendency to overemphasize information when it aligns with beliefs or values and ignore information that conflicts with them. Some students think they cannot make a decision unless they have *all* the information needed. Advisors can help them decide when they have enough. Students can also get side-tracked while searching information sources and go off on tangents that have nothing to do with the problem. Advisors can help students stay "on track" by helping them sort through information that is relevant and information that may be interesting but not useful in their situation.

Decision-Making Style. Advisors must be able to recognize decision-making styles, including their own. Logic and intuition are used to a certain degree in most decisions. The computer, with its capability of churning information into a logical, organized product, has made logic a natural part of decision making. Advisors (left-brain) who employ a predominantly logical approach to decision making may need to nurture their use of intuition in some situations. Advisors (right-brain) who use intuition or how a situation "feels" may need to use more logic as they approach the problem-solving process.

Advisors also need to be aware of whether they tend to make decisions externally or internally. External decision makers need to talk out loud about decisions, while others prefer to process information internally. Advisors need to be aware that students process information on these two dimensions. If an advisor prefers to discuss information verbally but works with a student who needs to process it internally before speaking, there might be a lack of adequate communication.

Advisor's Role. The advisor's role of problem solver requires skills that are both intuitive and learned. Since some students have had little experience in solving career-related problems, the advisor may need to assume the role of "problem-solving" teacher. Basic advisor questions include:

- How do students define their problems?
- What relevant career information do they have?
- What information do they still need?
- What other factors are pertinent to this situation?
- What outcomes do they desire?

Career-advising questions are often proffered in the context of academic queries, and since the two are intertwined it is sometimes difficult to separate them. For example, a premed student who is not performing well in organic chemistry may be rethinking her original goal. An advisor can help the student look at all the possible scenarios and help her identify possible alternative actions (for example, drop chemistry and retake it, get tutoring, explore other majors). Advisors must always be sensitive to the emotional content of certain dilemmas that students bring to them. In the example just given, the student may have many personal concerns about her goal of becoming a physician that need to be acknowledged and dealt with. Understanding the decision-making process and their own styles of approaching problem solving can help advisors become more sensitive to how students may perceive their problems and act on them.

Communication Competency

Most advisors have excellent competence in communicating with their students. There is a need, however, to continually monitor their communication skills and continually refine them. Advisors are aware that good communication skills include establishing rapport; being a sensitive, nonthreatening listener; conveying a strong level of acceptance and support; as well as clarifying and paraphrasing what a student has said. Occasionally advisors find themselves in situations where confrontation may be needed. Pointing out inconsistencies or unrealistic thinking to a student is not always pleasant, but when a certain level of trust exists between advisor and advisee, this communication technique may prove to be more effective.

Referral Competency

Making referrals to campus or community resources is another area where most advisors are fairly competent. This presumes that advisors have a thorough knowledge of the resources available to students. As advisors refer students, they need to (1) explain why the referral is made, (2) be aware of students' reaction to the referral (for example, their agreement for the need, their intent to follow up), and (3) indicate what specific services will be provided and who will be providing them. Advisors can also help the student formulate possible questions to ask. Depending on the student's reaction to the referral or his or her stress level, helping the student make contact with the resource or service while in the advisor's office may be needed in certain situations (for example, a referral for personal counseling).

Schein, Laff, and Allen (2004) state that "advice givers can help students coordinate their use of a variety of campus experts. For instance, advice givers can teach students how to use career specialists, working professionals, and reference librarians to investigate how career possibilities and personal interests fit into the fields of study students are trying to construct" (p. 29).

Making referrals to career services is an extremely important aspect of career advising, and sometimes advisors need to teach students how to use the resources to which they are referring. Before a referral is made it is important that students' concerns are clearly identified and that students take part in deciding the best resources for helping to resolve their particular problem. Effective referral skills ensure that students are using the full range of institutional and community resources that are available to them.

Teaching Competency

Teaching, like communication and referral, is a natural part of academic advising, but is a role that is often taken for granted. The qualities of a good teacher are also those of a good advisor. Both treat students as eager learners, not as receptacles into which information is poured. Both help students to analyze, synthesize, and evaluate information. In teaching and advising, what is being learned must be personalized from both the advisor's and the student's perspectives.

Teaching competence is especially vital in career advising, since the importance of assimilating information and learning often requires students to research and study. Advisors can teach students where to find information sources, research what they find, and analyze what they have learned. Students can also be encouraged to take an active role in their learning and evaluate how and what they are learning in the context of making career-related decisions. Good teachers give regular feedback, reinforcement, and encouragement to their students. Since career exploration is not always a priority with students, regular encouragement can keep the process moving in a positive direction.

Mentoring Competency

Advisors in disciplines for which there is a direct relationship between the major and occupational fields (for example, allied health areas, civil engineering, elementary education) may find themselves in the role of career mentor. Although not generally regarded as a part of academic advising, some advising relationships may develop into career mentoring, especially when the teaching role is incorporated. Communicating as a mentor may involve a more personal way of listening, asking questions, reflecting back feeling, and guiding conversation. A career mentor offers feedback and makes suggestions for approaching and solving career problems. Career mentoring may involve exposing the mentee to new opportunities, coaching, or even sponsoring them for an educational or work experience (Mentoring Leadership and Resource Network, 2003).

Career Assessment Competency

As detailed in Chapter 6, the advisor's role in career testing is limited to being knowledgeable about career methods and information resources so that proper referrals can be made. Advisors should be able to help students decide, for example, whether an interest inventory or another type of assessment might be useful in identifying occupational areas associated with their majors.

Assessment must be viewed as something that is done *with* students, not *to* them. Assessments should promote self-learning, and students should feel they own the results. Some advisors with the proper expertise will find it expedient to give certain students assessment instruments such as Holland's Self-Directed Search (SDS) to match majors and career fields for further exploration. Miller and Woycheck (2003), for example, describe the benefits to both students and their research efforts by using the SDS in their advising center. All students benefit when their advisors are knowledgeable about the assessment opportunities available on their campuses and can focus their referrals on the most personally relevant ones.

Technological Competency

How students adapt and learn from technology in college will affect how they will learn and succeed in the workplace. Bates and Poole (2003) indicate that "students need to learn how to use technology to seek, organize, analyze, and apply information appropriately. It will become increasingly difficult to accept someone as being fully educated if they do not know how to use the Internet to communicate with other professionals, if they do not know how to find Web sites that will provide relevant and reliable information within their field of study, or if they do not know how to develop their own multi-media reports for communicating their knowledge or research" (p. 9). We cannot expect students to understand the strengths and weaknesses of technology if teachers and advisors cannot use it effectively themselves.

Advisors are aware of the need to continually stay abreast of the technological changes on their campus and in the workplace in general. Most students today are very comfortable with technology, but advisors need to emphasize the importance of updating and acquiring new skills while in college. Technology increases the amount and ease with which advisors and students access career information. The Internet and computer-assisted guidance systems are incredible resources for this purpose. Advisors must be competent in guiding students to the technology needed to search for information as well as processing it effectively.

The National Forum on Information Literacy (2004) defines *information literacy* as a constellation of skills revolving around information research and use. The Forum outlines various areas of literacy, including:

Computer literacy: The ability to use a computer and its software to accomplish practical tasks

Technology literacy: The ability to use media such as the Internet to effectively access and communicate information

Information literacy: The ability to know when there is a need for information and to be able to identify, locate, evaluate, and effectively use that information for the issue or problem at hand

Media literacy: The ability to decode, analyze, evaluate, and produce communication in a variety of forms

These competencies can be considered the minimum literacy skills that advisors must be able to demonstrate as they use information in their administrative work as well as their work with students.

G. E. Steele (personal communication, September 6, 2005) projects that emerging technologies such as wireless video phones and cameras, course response systems (CRS) software, and collaborative learning environment (CLE) systems will have a significant effect on advising practices. CLE systems, for example, offer tracking capabilities that can help advisors monitor students' academic progress in real time. Advisors have greater access today to data that can be manipulated by complex tools in new software to create information and knowledge about their advisees. Steele suggests that the financial commitment that institutions make to advising technology in the future will depend on their perceptions of advising as essential to the institutional mission or just another service.

Advisors must also be alert to who is making and how decisions are being made on their campuses about adopting campus technology for advising (Steele, Miller, Steele, & Kennedy, 2005). The results of the National Survey on Technology in Academic Advising (Leonard, 2004) emphasize the need for periodic assessment of issues related to the policy and practice of technology in academic advising.

Evaluation Competency

The outcomes that advisors want to accomplish for themselves and their students involve the critical process of evaluation. As discussed in Chapter 1, it is important for advisors to create a list of goals for their advising practices. If a self-evaluation form does not exist, advisors should create one, listing the goals that they think are important to accomplish, including the area of career advising. Periodic evaluation will help to identify the goals that are being met and those that require new additions or changes. Advising is a fluid process, so it is necessary to check periodically whether desired outcomes are being achieved.

The checklist of advising questions offered in Chapter 1 is an example of outcomes that could be used in a self-evaluation. Many of the items in Checklist 1.1 can be viewed as action steps that can lead to enhanced advisor competencies in the career domain. The CAS standards mentioned in Chapter 1 (Council for the Advancement of Professional Standards for Higher Education, 2003) can also be used as guidelines for establishing personal career-advising goals. Whatever goals are set must be obtainable and measurable. Individual advisors will need to reflect on what is important to accomplish within the parameters of their own career-advising expertise.

Research Competency

The competence of advisors in research skills varies dramatically. The interest and competence that advisors might have in performing academic advising research will depend on many factors. Padak, Kuhn, Gordon, Steele, and Robbins (2005) maintain that every academic advisor is a potential researcher, and every researcher could profit from collaboration with practicing advisors.

Habley (2000) exhorts advisors to take the necessary steps to establish their own research bases, especially advisors who are in graduate programs and could focus on advising topics for their theses or dissertations. He also suggests that advisors become consumers of advising research by reading and understanding how to separate good from bad. He encourages faculty to center some of their research interests in academic advising. Advisors can share information about National Academic Advising Association (NACADA) grants and offer researchable advising questions with other advisors.

Padak et al. (2005) encourage the establishment of "research mentors" who would share their research expertise with advisors who have solid ideas for research studies but may not have the level of expertise needed. It is critically important that research become a high priority for advisors, because it will improve their advising practices when they engage in formal and informal research activities. Chapter 7 offers more suggestions for becoming involved in research efforts.

Amundson, Harris-Bowlsbey, and Niles (2005) use the competencies required by the National Career Development Association to examine the process of career counseling and techniques for helping students make appropriate occupational decisions. As stated in Chapter 1, implicit in the CAS standards for academic advising are the competencies advisors need to help students clarify, specify, and implement academic and career-related challenges and changes. How the competencies described earlier can be encompassed in advisor development programs is expanded upon next.

Advisor Development Programs

It is evident from the competencies described in the first part of the chapter that advisors must be continually involved in their own development if career-advising knowledge and skills are to be maintained and refined. Next, suggestions are offered for each of the competencies.

Theoretical Competency

- Assign each advisor a theory to research, report back to the group and lead a group discussion on how the theory can be applied to their daily work with students.

- Invite a faculty member who is an expert in career or student development theory to share his or her expertise with the group.
- Assign readings about a theory to the advising staff and lead a discussion during a staff meeting about the practical applications of the theory.

Decision-Making Competency

- Administer a decision-making style instrument to the staff and lead a discussion about different styles that are used in advising interactions.
- Search the *NACADA Journal* (via the NACADA Clearinghouse Web site) and copy several articles about career decision making for staff discussion.
- Invite a faculty member from the business department to discuss decision-making theory and its various applications.

Communication Competency

- Videotape volunteer advisors and students in a career-advising session and discuss how basic communication skills are used.
- Ask the campus counseling office to offer a workshop on communication and counseling skills.

Referral Competency

- Invite a professional from campus career services to discuss how students are assisted and the resources that are available.
- Arrange a staff meeting at the campus career library and give advisors an assignment that requires them to use the library's printed or computer resources.
- Ask advisors to use the computer information guidance system on campus and use their printouts as a career-advising exercise with a colleague.

Teaching Competency

- Pair advisors in role playing, teaching students to use career resources on the Internet.
- Teach a class in the career-planning course on campus on the academic relationship to career exploration.
- Lead a discussion on "advising as teaching" and how this can be applied to career exploration.

Mentoring Competency

- Develop mentoring policies that define mentoring relationships and when they are appropriate.
- Offer a workshop on mentoring techniques and skills.

Assessment Competency

- Ask a campus career counselor to discuss the various career tests that are offered at the career services office and what they measure.
- Take the Self-Directed Search (Holland, 1997) and discuss how it can be used in advising. Code all your academic majors according to Holland's codes.
- Take a work values inventory and discuss the values implicit in various academic and career fields.

Technology Competency

- Review and evaluate the policy in your advising unit about the use of e-mail in advising practices; if none exists, encourage your unit to develop one.
- Demonstrate your competencies in the information literacy skills (listed on p. 38) and, if needed, develop an action plan to improve or refine them.
- Identify the "decision makers" on your campus who are responsible for adopting technology for advising; invite them

to discuss with campus advisors their vision for the future of advising technology and how it will impact advising practices; add your vision to theirs.

Evaluation Competency

- Develop a personal philosophy of career advising that can guide the manner in which behavior and conduct is measured; share this philosophy and how to identify and evaluate possible outcomes with colleagues.

- Create a list of personal career-advising goals that describes what is important to accomplish when working with students in the career domain; compare with a colleagues' list.

- If a self-evaluation form does not exist, create one as a group project.

Research Competency

- Brainstorm different career-advising research ideas during a departmental or staff meeting and frame research questions in small groups; follow up with those who are interested in doing a research study.

- Invite a faculty member who teaches research design to provide a workshop for advisors.

- Invite a staff member from the department of institutional research to present information about the kind of support that is available to researchers on campus.

- Obtain information about NACADA research grants from its Web site and share this information with colleagues.

These are only a few of the unlimited possibilities for advisor development in the area of career advising. Workshops, staff meetings, focus groups, campus tours, and graduate courses are just a few of the methods for expanding advisors' awareness and expertise in career development, career information, and career decision making.

When advisors consciously try to improve their career-advising techniques, other advising practices will benefit as well. Advisor competencies need to be continually improved and updated. Any of the competences described in this chapter can become the focus of faculty or staff advisors' development sessions or adopted as a competency for improvement by individual advisors as part of their evaluation.

Summary

Although career advising does not require different methods and techniques from academic advising, certain advisor competencies are emphasized and expanded. The need to be familiar with career information sources, for example, requires extended knowledge of occupational information and the variety of sources for accessing it. This chapter has described nine advisor competencies that are emphasized in career advising.

These competencies are the foundation for integrating career information and advice into academic advising practice. The next chapters describe how these competencies can be put into practical use when advisors engage in career advising.

3

THE 3-I PROCESS

A Career-Advising Framework

Advisors are familiar with students who are in various places on their ways to thinking and deciding about their academic and career-related futures. All students are in some stage of academic and career planning, that is, they are in various phases of exploration and decision making. Some are just beginning to think about the career and life decisions they will need to make, while others are taking action to implement the ones to which they have made a commitment. How students go through these developmental phases during their college years is unique to the individual.

This chapter and the next two outline a career-advising framework that entails three aspects of the career-advising process. The *3-I Process* integrates the career component into academic advising. INQUIRE, INFORM, and INTEGRATE are natural phases in the academic and career decision-making process. (See Figure 3.1.)

The 3-I Process is based on many decision-making frameworks but most closely resembles that of a theoretical construct developed by Tiedeman and O'Hara (1963). These theorists espoused a paradigm for decision making that includes a planning stage and an action stage. In the planning stage, students move through *exploration*, where they have vague ideas about the future, have no plan of action as yet, and no negative choices. As they move into the *crystallization* stage, they are making progress toward a choice, begin to recognize alternatives, and weigh the advantages and disadvantages of each. They eventually make a definite commitment in the *choice* stage and feel satisfied and relieved. They also consider the consequences of their decision and begin further planning. In

Figure 3.1   The 3-I Process

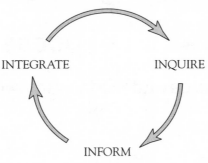

INTEGRATE   INQUIRE

INFORM

the planning stage, students engage in the process of closure about their commitments and plan the details and next steps that need to be implemented. Students' self-images and images of the future are elaborated and perfected. The 3-I Process encompasses the planning stages of Tiedeman and O'Hara's paradigm. Although not included, Tiedeman and O'Hara's action stage involves individuals living out their decisions by becoming part of the new environments they have chosen (for example, college or workplace). They begin to identify with their new environments by assimilation of the environment's values and goals; become highly involved and interact assertively, not passively, in the new environment; and eventually synthesize the group's purposes with their own. This whole process of planning and action, according to Tiedeman and O'Hara, is ordinarily progressive, but regression and recycling are possible. It is important to understand that the different phases in the 3-I Process are fluid and flexible.

In the 3-I Process, students might bring academic and career concerns in any of these three phases:

1. Student A is the questioning phase (INQUIRE) as he begins to realize that certain academic and career decisions will need to be made. This transition often triggers questions and concerns about future academic and career planning.

2. Student B understands that she needs information (INFORM) about many aspects of the career choice process. She wants to know what information she needs, where she can find it, and how she can use it.

3. Student C has all the information he needs and is in the process of solving a career problem or making a career-related decision. He needs help in pulling together all the disparate pieces (INTEGRATE). He also needs to implement the decision he has made.

Although all students in time pass through all these processes, they may contact advisors while engaged in any of them. For example, advisors may use only the INQUIRE process with students who are just beginning the exploration process. Advisors may need to help other students through two processes, INFORM and INTEGRATE, as they begin to gather information and then need assistance in making sense of what they have learned. Advisors need to recognize the phase in which each student is engaged and adjust their approach accordingly.

The next three chapters suggest the type of career concerns that students might bring to these different stages of career exploration and planning. Advisor responses are suggested for each part of the process. The 3-I Process should not be viewed as rigid or linear. It designates three interactive phases that students might be passing through as they explore different academic and career possibilities, make decisions, and begin to implement them.

INQUIRE

The INQUIRE phase of the decision-making process involves identifying students' academic and career concerns, clarifying their needs, and making appropriate responses that help them move to the information-collecting phase. Academic advisors expect students to ask them questions. How advisors listen, interpret, and answer questions effectively is an art. For example, a student may want to drop a course because of financial stress, family problems, or failure in a course. Each of these reasons prompts a different set of questions that advisors might ask to clarify the student's situation. Each of these reasons has implications for the student's academic status, personal life, or career goals. Failing required courses in some competitive majors may mean a student needs to rethink his or her choice. Financial or family problems may lead to a delay in rescheduling a course sequence in some career preparation curricula, such as nursing or architecture. Although advisors are usually astute in discussing the academic implications of dropping a course, they also need to consider how it might affect the student's career plans and goals.

Academic advisors are in an ideal position to help students understand the relationships between their academic and career decisions and the impact these decisions have on their futures. Career advising is not just helping English majors identify possible jobs that might appeal to their interests and abilities. Career advising encompasses the whole realm of factors that students confront as they make academic choices that will influence future career-related opportunities. Some academic decisions not only have an impact on students' immediate college experiences but their future lifestyles as well.

Many academic advisors are aware of students who have chosen a particular major because they think it will lead directly to a job after college. Some parents encourage their students to select these areas because the parents are concerned about security or good salaries. Such jobs, of course, don't always work out. Some students change majors and must rethink their academic and career goals. Students who are undecided about a major when they enter college may hesitate to select the ones they are interested in because the job connections aren't obvious. When academic advisors don't acknowledge the major-occupation connection in students' thinking, they miss an opportunity to become full partners in the academic decision-making process. The bridges need to be built, and advisors can be the initial support for doing so. There are as many career questions as there are students asking them. Some possible career-related questions and advisor responses are offered in this chapter.

Career Concerns

In the real world of advising, there are different types of advisor-student contacts and settings. Some advisors experience the one-stop or "McAdvising" situation. When students ask career-related questions, it is often tempting to refer them immediately to the career services on campus. It is important at this juncture to ask students to return when more time is available or refer them to a campus resource when the problem demands immediate attention. Career concerns, whether simple or complex, should never be ignored.

Advisors who are fortunate to work with a student on a long-term basis or have more time to work with others during appointments have an opportunity to engage in career advising in more depth. Career concerns are not always obvious but may emerge as students share their reasons for requesting academic help. *Given the time constraints on most advisors' time, it is imperative that they become proficient in identifying core career-related concerns from the questions students ask.*

Career-related problems fall into at least three general areas: information deficits, general indecision, and personal concerns. Some examples follow.

Information Deficits

Students may:

- Be unable to relate occupational information to their current academic major
- Lack information about occupational fields in general
- Ask what kind of job they can get with their major
- Don't know how or where to access career information

- Be unable to choose between two strong alternative majors or career fields because of lack of information

General Indecision

Students may:

- Be developmentally not "ready" (that is, lack career maturity) to engage in the tasks involved in academic and career exploration and decision making
- Need to assess their strengths and limitations as they relate to career fields
- Be unable to relate what they know about themselves to career fields
- Change major because they no longer want the career field to which it leads
- Lack general decision-making experiences and skills
- Be unable to set career goals

Personal Concerns

Students may:

- Have difficulty picturing themselves in a work environment (vocational self-concept)
- Lack confidence in performing decision-making tasks (self-efficacy)
- Lack motivation to explore career alternatives
- Be encumbered with occupational stereotypes, thus eliminating viable career fields
- Experience parental pressures to choose an unwanted career direction
- Be indecisive decision makers

It is obvious that some of these concerns, such as those related to indecisiveness or obvious levels of high stress or depression, are not within the purview of academic advising. A problem for some advisors is knowing *when* to refer, especially when it pertains to career-related problems that are more personal in nature. Some stated career concerns may disguise a personal concern that the student is consciously (or unconsciously) covering up. Other students may need help with family or more personal problems that are impinging on their career decision-making processes. Advisors should sense when they are ill equipped to help students solve more personally related career problems. At times they must rely on their instincts (as they do with more personal academic concerns) to determine if the problems are severe enough to warrant referral to a personal counselor. The best adage may be when in doubt, refer.

Advising Nontraditional or Special Needs Students

It hardly needs to be said that today's campuses reflect the diverse populations that make up our current society. The career concerns of different types of students are as diverse as the students themselves. Although for many years campus career services were designed for traditional-age undergraduate students, these services have changed dramatically over the past few decades.

It is always dangerous to generalize about specific groups of students since individuals often differ within a group even though environmental and cultural differences are similar. Each student brings a distinctive set of characteristics and backgrounds that place his or her career concerns into their particular context. Although this applies to all students, some examples of students who may bring more specific concerns to the career-advising process follow.

Cultural and Ethnic Considerations

DeVaney and Hughey (2000) indicate that racial identity influences the vocational process in terms of "career maturity, perceptions of racial climate, work adjustment, and work satisfaction" (p. 234). It has little impact, however, on content variables such as needs, interests, or college major. Cultural differences exert strong influences on some ethnic minority students' career choices as well as their decision-making styles.

African American Students. According to Sharf (1997), African Americans are "less likely to envision themselves in particular occupations, perceive a more limited range of appropriate jobs, and are less likely to take ownership of their career decisions" (p. 239). Faculty mentoring programs have had a positive effect on minority academic achievement and retention (Campbell & Campbell, 1997) and faculty advisors are important sources of both academic and career information. DeVaney and Hughey (2000) recommend that advising in a broader life-planning process rather than a narrow occupational focus can help African American students acquire planning skills that will transfer into other family and worker roles.

Asian American Students. Although Asian American students are from many cultures, they share a common worldview. Generally they place a high value on occupational prestige, financial success, and job security. This causes some Asian American students to not consider certain occupations, such as teaching, law, and politics (DeVaney & Hughey, 2000). Mau (2004) found that Asian American students perceived more difficulty with career decision making than other groups, while White Americans perceived the fewest difficulties. She concluded that individual-oriented cultures are more conducive to fostering independent, rational approaches to career decision making than are collective-oriented cultures.

Career indecision in Asian American women, according to Sharf (1997), may stem from a lack of vocational information and role models. They may experience internal conflict when they consider career fields that are personally appealing but culturally inappropriate. Sharf suggests advisors help them develop study and decision-making skills, build confidence, and consider a broad range of occupational fields. According to Leong (1986), Asian American students may present academic and career issues to their faculty advisors when the real concerns are interpersonal in nature.

Hispanic Students.   Hispanic students' attitudes toward work are similar to those of White students when they enter college, but expectations for success and occupational aspirations tend to decline later (DeVaney & Hughey, 2000). Advisors must recognize the strong influence of traditional cultural values, especially family expectations, when helping Hispanic students make academic and career choices.

Since familial and societal expectations often influence career decisions, making a choice is not always done by the individual but by many people (for example, family, friends, significant others). Some minority students may consider a narrower range of occupations because they are considered inappropriate in their culture. Some are less likely to take ownership of their career decisions, as well. Advisors also need to be aware that a future orientation is not a cultural value shared by all students (Carter, 1991). A focus needs to be on career information; when advisors help students use the Internet to search for information, they may be teaching valuable technology skills as well.

Brown (2000) points out that one very important factor in advising minorities is language. Linguists have documented important differences among cultures in both verbal and nonverbal communication: "Rapidity of speech, verbal expressiveness, use of interpersonal space, tolerances for silence and many other variables differ across cultures" (p. 373). Minority students who persist in college tend to interact more extensively with faculty than White students interact with faculty (Sharf, 1997). Faculty advisors have an excellent opportunity to address career concerns and issues in these contacts.

Other Special Needs Students

There are many other special needs students who by virtue of their unique situations require different types of career information and advice. People with learning and other disabilities have been part of higher education for many years, but there has been a surge in enrollments in the past fifteen years (Hitchings & Retish, 2000). Zunker (2001) lists some of the special problems of disabled students, such as social/interpersonal skills, attitudinal barriers, lack of role models, and self-concept. Although many advisors refer their disabled advisees to the appropriate campus resources, they might also refer them to the excellent information that the U.S. government provides about how specific occupations will accommodate their specific disability (http://www.disabilityinfo.gov).

Adult students return to college for many reasons, many of them career related. Since adults have supposedly gained knowledge from previous experience, it might be assumed they need little help. Some research has shown, however, that they are similar to traditional-age students in their knowledge of career decision principles, knowledge of preferred occupations, and level of career indecision (Luzzo, 2000). Advisors need to be aware of the multiple roles older students play and the work, family, and community responsibilities they are juggling in addition to their college work. Adult students need academic advice throughout the term, advice about prior learning assessment, and help in negotiating the academic process when family or career interferes with academic progress (Banta, Hansen, Black, & Jackson, 2002). Responding to career concerns may require e-mail or telephone contact, but many adult students might appreciate referrals to specific academic- and career-related Web sites or other online resources.

Federal laws and executive orders bar discrimination in employ-ment based on race, color, religion, sex, national origin, age, and handicap. Niles and Harris-Bowlsbey (2002) warn that "many women, people of color, persons with disabilities, gay/lesbian/bisex-ual individuals regularly experience discrimination practices in hir-ing and promoting, insufficient financial resources, and a lack of role models and mentors" (p. 99). Advisors who work with students with discrimination concerns should be aware of the information and other campus resources that can help them.

Communicating

Regardless of the type of student or the type of career concern that needs to be addressed, communicating with students is at the heart of advising. It has been said that 90 percent of a working day is spent in some form of communication, such as listening, speaking, writing, and reading. Advisors may be the most informed people on campus in certain areas, but if they cannot communicate effectively, their knowledge will not be useful. Good communicators are able to:

- Concentrate on what the student is saying
- Screen out distractions
- Focus on nonverbal messages
- Listen for the key points the student is trying to make
- Reflect back the main ideas that are presented
- Respond to the student with interest and empathy
- Listen and respond to any emotions being expressed
- Listen in a patient, nonthreatening manner
- Go beyond the surface meaning of words
- Suggest possible actions the student might take

As advisors work with students who have career-related concerns, there are certain communication skills that are especially important.

Listening

Effective listening is a critical skill, especially in today's technological world. *How* students present their concerns is as important as the words they use. Tone and inflection of voice as well as nonverbal movements reveal a great deal about a student's feelings and attitudes. Listening requires being sensitive to the meaning behind the words, since there can be layers of meaning behind a simple question or sentence. As advisors listen to students' concerns, they are automatically assigning meaning to the words and formulating questions to clarify what they are hearing. They also need to listen for the career content implicit in what students are expressing. At times even students are not aware of the career implications of their questions until advisors call them to their attention.

Questioning

For some expressed concerns, only a simple solution is required. But as most advisors are aware, one question may raise many more questions. Questioning, like listening, requires skill. Advisors can ask questions for information or to clarify what the student has said. In many situations, questioning beyond the surface problem may uncover facts and emotions that students might hesitate to reveal at first. Advisors must also be sensitive to and refrain from asking questions the student is not ready to answer. This is especially important with minority students, since some may have cultural issues with self-disclosure (Sue & Sue, 1990).

   To summarize, much of the communication between an advisor and student involves identifying a problem, exchanging information, and arriving at a resolution. This process may take five minutes, an hour, a week, or even more. In the time-restrictive environment in which many advisors work, there is a tendency to provide answers too quickly without involving the student in the process. *How* information is relayed is as important as the information itself. Although advisors may not always want to delve too deeply into some issues, they should never ignore those that might have a real impact on the student's academic and career situation.

Technology

A great deal of communication between advisor and student today is done through technology. Ninety-five percent of all college students access the Internet on a weekly basis and spend at least twenty hours a week online (http://wordofmouse.com).

Steele and Gordon (2001) found that, overall, most advisors profess a positive attitude about performing advising duties by e-mail but that 69 percent of the academic units within which the advisor respondents worked had no policies regarding the use of technology in advising.

Some advisors establish a listserv or an e-mail program so their advisees can ask questions or share concerns. They can provide career information links on their Web sites and offer career-related information through e-mail newsletters and electronic bulletin boards. Advisors can also assist students who are requesting career information by helping them search over the Internet (Sotto, 2000). Providing a list of career Web sites relevant to their academic major can not only offer sources of helpful information but will encourage students to take responsibility for their own exploration.

Advisor Questions

Advisors are often the first professionals on campus to hear a student express a career concern. Who else on campus is in a more advantageous place in intercepting students who have no one to talk to about their career thoughts and plans and don't know where to go for help? Advisors can act as a sounding board to help students think through all the ramifications of their problem and possible ways to resolve it. Just as important is how they refer students to a career resource so that it is targeted to the student's specific, timely need.

When advisors sense that their students are struggling with career decisions, they may want to ask a series of questions. Examples of questions advisors might ask in the areas of self-knowledge, occupational information, and decision making follow.

Self-Knowledge Questions

- What are some career fields that interest you?
- Are you having difficulty in identifying your interests? What would help you do this?
- Do you have so many interests that none stand out? Which ones have you identified?
- Have you used any career resources to explore your interests (for example, interest inventories, computer-based systems, extracurricular activities, work experiences)? Which ones?
- What are your strongest abilities (identified, for example, from good coursework grades, talents, work-related experiences, hobbies, leisure activities)? Why do you consider these strong?
- What do you value? What is important to you in a job? (See Checklist 3.1 for a list of work values.) Why?
- How do these values match the occupations you are considering?
- What kind of work experience have you had (for example, summer jobs, part-time employment, volunteer work)? What did you learn from it?
- Are you feeling pressure to make a certain decision to please other people whose opinions you respect? If so, how is it affecting your decision making?
- What if anything is standing in your way of making a commitment to a major?

Occupational Information Questions

- What information have you collected so far about (*occupation*)?

Checklist 3.1   *GOE* Work Values

Check the five work values that are most important to you in a job:

____ 1. *Ability Utilization:* Making use of your individual abilities

____ 2. *Achievement:* Getting a feeling of accomplishment

____ 3. *Activity:* Being busy all the time

____ 4. *Authority:* Giving directions and instructions to others

____ 5. *Autonomy:* Planning your work with little supervision

____ 6. *Coworkers:* Having coworkers who are easy to get along with

____ 7. *Company Policies and Procedures:* Being treated fairly by the company

____ 8. *Compensation:* Being paid well in comparison with other workers

____ 9. *Creativity:* Trying out your own ideas

____ 10. *Independence:* Doing your work alone

____ 11. *Moral Values:* Never being pressured to do things that go against your sense of right and wrong

____ 12. *Recognition:* Receiving recognition for the work you do

____ 13. *Responsibility:* Making decisions on your own

____ 14. *Security:* Having steady employment

____ 15. *Social Service:* Doing things for other people

____ 16. *Social Status:* Being looked up to by others in your company or in your community

____ 17. *Supervision, Human Relations:* Having supervisors who back you with management

____ 18. *Supervision, Technical:* Having supervisors who train you well

____ 19. *Working Conditions:* Having good working conditions

---

Note: These values are taken from Farr, Ludden, and Shatkin (2001), pp. 448–452. The *Guide for Occupational Exploration* can be obtained from JIST Works (http://www.jist.com). Work values are listed with the fourteen corresponding work groups.

- Where did you find the information?
- How do you know the information is accurate, up to date?
- With whom have you discussed it?
- What conclusions have you drawn from the information?
- What information do you still need in order to resolve the problem?

- What resources will help you find it?
- What are you going to do with this information once you collect it?

Decision-Making Questions

- How do you usually make decisions (for example, systematically, spontaneously, rationally, intuitively)?
- Can you describe a decision you have made in the past two weeks and how you made it?
- Do you need to talk to others before you can make a decision? To whom do you share your ideas and how do they help you?
- What values are important to you in this decision?
- How well do you integrate your values into your decision making?
- How do you differentiate between a good decision and a bad one?
- What outcomes would you like as a result of the decision you are currently trying to make?
- What action steps will you take to implement your decision once it is made?
- How do you set goals for yourself? Do you usually meet them? Give an example.
- What academic and career goals have you set for yourself? How will you fulfill them?

By asking these types of questions, a clearer picture of the student's career concern can be determined. How the student answers will reveal what the student has done to resolve the problem so far, and what parts of the problems still need to be addressed. Advisors can help students determine what actions need to be taken to move the process along or resolve it.

Inquiring not only involves questions that students ask, but also the questions that advisors ask in response. The questioning phase is sometimes taken for granted since it is such a natural part of communicating. This is a critical part of the career-advising process because:

- It establishes the nature of the relationship between advisor and student.
- It portrays the advisor as a caring person who is interested in the student's career as well as academic concerns.
- It establishes the advisor as a reliable resource for career information.
- It sets up the communication patterns necessary for problem solving.
- It determines whether a specific career concern requires a simple or more detailed approach to resolving it.
- It ferrets out the problems that might be below the surface but need to be addressed.

Much of advising is problem solving, and questioning is its first step. John Dewey (1910) offered some steps in problem solving:

1. A difficulty is felt.
2. Difficulty is located and defined.
3. Possible solutions are suggested.
4. Consequences are considered.
5. A solution is accepted.

Dewey's first step involves *feelings* and his last step involves *acceptance*. Although a linear model, his steps in problem solving include the other important elements of questioning, information gathering, and identifying solutions and their consequences.

Summary

The proposed framework for career advising used in this book consists of three phases that, while flowing into one another, offer a sequence of tasks in which students are involved as they solve career problems and make decisions. A student's first contact with an advisor about a career concern will usually begin with questions. Advisors' responsibility at this point is to help students clarify their concerns by asking probing questions so that both advisor and student can begin to address the problem precisely. After the INQUIRE phase, advisors and students move into the INFORM aspect of the career-advising process, where the focus is on gathering and processing information. Advisors may find some students are just beginning to need help in identifying and gathering the kind of information they need, while others have all the information required, but need assistance in INTEGRATING it into a coherent whole. Chapter 4 concentrates on helping students identify the information they need, where to find it, and how to process it within their personal context.

4

THE 3-I PROCESS

INFORM

The acquisition and effective use of educational and career *information* is an integral part of academic advising. Three areas where students need to gather career information are (1) their personal attributes, such as their likes and dislikes, their strongest abilities, and their values; (2) educational information, such as how academic decisions (for example, major, coursework) relate to possible career directions and the acquisition of marketable skills; and (3) the type of occupational information that is pertinent to their academic situation and career goals. When these areas are integrated, more coherent, informed, realistic decisions are likely to be made. This is a difficult task but one where advisors can make a difference in how successfully students move through the information-gathering process.

Many students want and expect their advisors to be experts in educational and career information and think that learning about the jobs that majors prepare them for is the most important career strategy they can take. At its most basic level, career information can be a collection of facts, but facts are not very helpful if they are not applied or integrated into students' personal characteristics, such as their interest patterns, their current academic records, and their aspirations. In a study by Reinarz and Ehrlich (2002), students reported they received more information from their advisors than when they just read about it. They were also more apt to take action after an advising session. Advisors play a critical role in providing information and helping students learn how to use it when scheduling courses, choosing majors, and exploring a wide array of career fields related to their academic interests.

Self-Information

Some personal areas that are considered important in gathering information are interests, abilities, skills, and values. Some examples of situations when students may need to connect personal information with career information and suggestions for advisor responses are presented in the following sections.

Interests

Interests are "those things a person does for fun or enjoys" (Reardon, Lenz, Sampson, & Peterson, 2000, p. 27). Interests are developed through exposure to areas of activity, including experiences with family, friends, school, and leisure. Students' interests usually reflect their competencies and what is important to them. Some people have a wide range of interests, while others' interests are more limited in scope. Interests change as new ones are formed and old ones are discarded. Work that incorporates one's interests and allows individuals to follow their passions will probably enhance career satisfaction.

Students who need to explore their interest patterns might present the following concerns when deciding on a major or career field.

Examples of Student Concerns

Student A: "I'm not sure what I am interested in; nothing stands out."

Student B: "I have so many interests that I can't narrow them down."

Student C: "I know what I'm interested in but I don't know how they connect to jobs."

Even though Student A may not be aware of it, she probably has preferred interests in certain coursework, leisure time activities, or work-related tasks. Her advisor might suggest that she view a list of work activities so she can identify a few for further study. Student B might benefit from an interest inventory in which he will identify and prioritize certain activities over others. Student C needs information that can help him make that important connection between interests and occupational fields. Interest inventories, for example, can provide lists of career fields that match certain interest patterns.

Advisor Response. Since Student A cannot identify her interests, she needs a more structured approach. One possible method is an interest card sort that her advisor can create herself (see Chapter 6 for a detailed description). The campus career office can provide many resources for determining students' interest patterns. In addition to print interest inventories, many career centers offer computer-assisted career guidance programs through which students can take inventories of their interests, values, abilities, and skills. A profile of the student's interests and strengths is integrated into a major and occupational database. The student can then select specific occupations that she wishes to explore further. This would be especially useful to Students B and C, since they could access occupational information from an extensive computer database. Student B might benefit from both an interest and a values inventory, since he can prioritize occupations on two dimensions. A more detailed description of interest inventories, the card sort technique, computer-assisted career systems, and other information regarding interests is provided in Chapter 6.

Abilities and Skills

The terms *achievement, ability, aptitude, talent,* and *skill* can be confusing. Although these words are often used interchangeably, their meanings are different. *Achievement* is what a person has accomplished already (the past). The Scholastic Aptitude Test (SAT) and ACT test for example, measure what the student knows up to the point of taking the test. *Ability* is what a person is capable of performing now (the present). For example, a person may have the ability to manage a football team or cook a gourmet meal. *Aptitude* is the potential to learn (the future) and the ease with which it can be learned. The U.S. Department of Labor has identified the aptitudes, such as verbal, numerical, spatial, and manual dexterity, needed to perform certain work tasks. (For specific lists of aptitudes and the occupations using them, see *O*Net*, http://online.onetcenter.org.) *Talent* is a term that defines the natural endowment of a person to perform in a field or activity such as music or sports.

A *skill* is the ability to do something. Skills denote competence in an activity or task that can be learned. Examples of work skills are interpersonal skills, analytical skills, computer skills, leadership skills, or teamwork skills. A student stagehand in a theatre production on campus has the skills of building and repairing scenery, while a business student has the skills of managing and budgeting the production's money. *Transferable skills*, such as communicating, analyzing, and problem solving, are used in many occupations. Knotts (2002) urges liberal arts students to develop these "new economy" transferable skills through an academic plan that includes personal, educational, and career goals. He lists these skills as core liberal arts skills, research design skills, data analysis skills, computer application skills, and general business skills (also discussed in Chapter 7), and lists courses for acquiring these skills in many disciplines across the curricula.

Functional skills are those that are required to perform the work tasks in a specific occupation, such as the medical skills of diagnosing and prescribing that are needed by physicians. Students in majors that lead directly to occupational fields learn many of these skills during the course of their studies, but most people learn functional skills on the job. In many of today's workplaces, functional skills need to be continually updated.

Coplin (2003) surveyed the nation's top ten companies asking them to identify the essential skills necessary to keep workers marketable. Some of the skills he lists in his book, *10 Things Employers Want You to Learn in College*, are leadership, self-motivation, relationship building, information evaluation, and time management.

Examples of Student Concerns

Student A: "I thought I wanted engineering, but I didn't realize how much math is involved. I'm not sure I have the ability for engineering coursework."

Student B: "What kinds of skills are required to perform the work tasks in computer science?"

Student C: "I have artistic talent but I'm not sure I want to be an art major. What do I need to be a cartoonist?"

Student A is seriously considering changing his major because he is doing poorly in his engineering courses. Student B is interested in becoming a computer programmer, and she is interested in knowing what skills she will be using in that occupation. Student C is trying to decide on a major but is not sure how to pursue his interest in cartooning.

Advisor Response. Student A's advisor might want to ask why he chose engineering as a major. If his decision was based on informed, realistic information about what engineers do and his math capabilities, the advisor might suggest math tutoring or other resources, such as talking with practicing engineers. If the student is not sure he wants to stay in engineering, the advisor might help him begin a series of exploratory steps to either confirm his initial choice or identify some alternative majors. Student B needs occupational information. Her advisor can suggest some reliable information sources, such as the U.S. government's Web site *O*NET* or the *Occupational Outlook Handbook (OOH)*, which lists the skills needed to perform the work tasks in different occupations (see Chapters 5 and 6 for more detailed descriptions). Student C needs more information about the abilities and skills required in an area he is exploring to determine how his art ability will be used. Like Student B, he needs occupational information about all the possibilities in art career fields. The advisor and student need to discuss what methods and resources would provide the most relevant information.

Values

One of the most important personal characteristics associated with career planning is an individual's basic beliefs or values. Work values are those most important to consider when choosing a major or career field. Values motivate people to take action either to pursue an activity or avoid it. Interests and values both play an important part in determining career choice satisfaction.

Begley and Johnson (2000) urge advisors to consider a values perspective in their work. They suggest that advisors consciously develop sensitivity to their own value orientations as well as their students' and cultivate the development of their skills in this area. Advisors can help a student confirm a major or career choice by asking what the student values the most about it. Some students may have difficulty because they have a conflict between their career choices and their values. Certain values are implicit in certain career fields. For example, business students may express the values of variety, recognition, economic reward, influence, independence, or interaction, to name a few. Art students may express the values of creativity, expression, recognition, or influence. The *Guide for Occupational Exploration (GOE)* (2001) provides a crosswalk from fourteen work groups to work values. (The GOE values are listed in Checklist 3.1.) For example, under the work value of "Creativity: Trying out your own ideas," it lists the work groups of Writing and Editing, Visual Arts, Modeling and Personal Appearance, Engineering, and Managerial Work in Sales and Marketing.

Any list of work values can provide examples that advisors might use to show students who seem to be having difficulty identifying or clarifying their values. Discussing the values described in Checklist 3.1 could help them identify and prioritize the values they prefer in a work setting. A discussion about the values implicit in their majors or career alternatives will help to clarify what students consider the most important in each.

Examples of Student Concerns

Student A: "I'm a business major because I want a job that has a lot of variety and pays well."

Student B: "I love my ethnic studies major because it really challenges me intellectually; every course is interesting, but I don't know what jobs I can get with it."

Student C: "I'm an engineering major, but the more I think about it, the more I want to work with children."

Student A has expressed two values that she thinks will be met in a position in the business world. Student B is satisfied with his major because it meets his need to be intellectually stimulated. He needs to explore general occupational fields that might also reflect this value. Student C is expressing a possible conflict between her current major and the value she places on working with children.

Advisor Response. An advisor might commend Student A for realizing what she values in a job but point out it is sometimes difficult to realize all one's values in one job. Some well-paying jobs are dull; some jobs that are filled with a variety of tasks may not necessarily pay well. The advisor might help the student articulate more clearly how she defines these two values. Together they can explore the many occupations in business where these values might be found. Student B needs information about the values implicit in various occupations and might use resources such as the *GOE* list described in Checklist 3.1 or a computerized career guidance system, such as SIGI Plus, that can help her make the connections between her values and occupational fields. Student C needs to define her values more clearly or decide what is the most important to her in work. She would benefit from a values inventory as well.

Educational Information

In addition to self-information, the second general area where students need *information* is when they are making academic or general education decisions. Most academic advisors are experts in the academic information that pertains to their particular institution. The layers of coursework required by most four-year colleges and universities include the basic requirements that all students are expected to fulfill (for example, math, science, humanities, social sciences), departmental major requirements (for example, certain kinds of math courses and courses in the major itself), and other courses that might be required for graduation (for example, senior thesis, elective hours). Academic coursework required by community colleges will depend on the curriculum chosen (for example, technical degree, associate's degree) and the requirements of all the majors within their field at transfer schools in their region.

Selecting the right courses and staying on an academic plan are critical parts of being a successful student. A few students who are able to follow a highly structured curriculum as outlined in the college catalog may not visit an advisor very often. Other students with no particular goals may put together a schedule with courses that simply interest them. The majority of students, however, use a combination of institutional materials (for example, catalogs, Web sites) and the advice of their academic advisors when they schedule. *All* of these students need academic information that is timely, understandable, and clearly presented by an advisor.

Most advisors are comfortable working with students to chart a path through the maze of requirements the institution requires for graduation. Advisors also need to communicate the rationale for general education and prerequisite requirements for coursework as well as the different criteria for entering majors at their institutions. In some cases, clarifying or even interpreting what is written in the catalog may prevent some students from making mistakes that side-track or delay their graduation. Many advisors view the dispensing of academic information as their primary responsibility. Career information, however, adds another important dimension to educational planning and decision making.

Although academic advisors work primarily with college students, it is important for them to be familiar with information resources about other types of education. The U.S. Department of Labor describes educational programs that lead to different degrees (that is, bachelor's, technical, associate's, graduate, and professional). (See the *Occupational Outlook Handbook,* http://www.bls.gov/oco.) Some occupations require additional credentials such as licenses or certificates. A few students may feel misplaced in a four-year program, for example. Their goals and aspirations may be better fulfilled with a two-year technical degree. Many community college students, on the other hand, transfer to a four-year institution to complete a bachelor's degree. Some students consider college as preparation for the work world, while others place value on the opportunity to become generally educated. Most advisors are familiar with graduate or professional school opportunities that are related to their disciplines. Advisors need to be sensitive, however, to the reasons their advisees are in college and to students whose career aspirations might be fulfilled at another type or level of education.

Information about the educational levels required for the fastest-growing occupations is also provided in the U.S. Department of Labor's publication, the *Occupational Outlook Handbook (OOH)*. For example, the fast-growing occupations of computer support specialists and registered nurses require an associate's degree, while physical therapists and librarians are required to have a master's degree.

Preparation for the workplace should include a broad range of coursework that can help build transferable skills. Reardon, Lenz, Sampson, and Peterson (2000) suggest that general education courses can broaden students' appreciation of what is happening in the world that affects their work and lives: "Some experts have suggested that general knowledge, apart from technical skills and direct knowledge learned in the major, have a powerful impact on employment success" (p. 101). Although technical and job-related skills may be helpful in obtaining a job offer, general knowledge skills contribute more to long-term employment success.

Many students consider choosing a major the most important decision they make in college. Some get caught in the "chicken and egg" question: whether to choose a major and then search for career fields to which it might lead; or to choose an occupation and then find the major that will lead to it. Some majors can prepare students directly for work in a specific career field, such as teaching or physical therapy, but many graduates enter the job market in positions that have no direct relationship to their academic concentrations. This is a point that many liberal arts advisors make often to students. The myth of the importance of choosing the "right" major can be dispelled by pointing out to students the value of considering broad career fields rather than specific occupations.

The career-advising component of academic advising helps make the connection between academic and career information. Many students are interested in how the coursework they are taking might prepare them for their work lives after graduation. The future workplace will require that students acquire the skills needed to succeed in complex, changing, demanding work environments. This means advisors must be able to help students select the type of curriculum that takes advantage of their academic interests and strengths. Elective courses can also provide the opportunity for students to acquire skills that will enhance their employability. Career advising broadens students' perspective about the role a college education will play in their future lives.

Occupational Information

Gathering occupational information is a critical part of academic and career decision making. Information resources for this area are so varied and plentiful that beginning a search may seem overwhelming to some students. Often students don't know where to start because they (1) aren't sure what information they need, (2) don't know where to find it, and (3) don't know what to do with it once they have it. This is why an advisor's involvement is so important. Students need help in narrowing and prioritizing the alternatives that interest them. Once possible fields are identified, advisors can guide students to viable information resources (for example, printed, Internet, computer-assisted guidance systems) that will provide the type of information essential to making good decisions.

What information do advisors and students need to collect about an occupation when beginning a search? Sample questions include:

- What kind of work is performed? What work tasks are involved?
- What personal qualifications are required?
- What are the working conditions like?
- What are the earnings and benefits?
- What kind of education and training is needed for entry and advancement?
- What academic majors might be connected to this occupation?
- What are some related occupations in the same field?
- What is the future employment outlook?

These questions lead to gathering the basic information that students need to know about the *nature of work* (specific work tasks involved); *places of employment* (for example, business, industry, health areas, nonprofits); *qualifications and advancement* (for example, are licensing, credentialing required?); *earnings and working conditions* (for example, beginning salaries, where does work take place?); and *employment outlook* (what are the projections for the job market four or five years from now?). Collecting basic information about job-seeking skills is also important.

Advisors don't need to be encyclopedias of career information, but they do need to know what information is relevant to their particular advisees and where to locate it efficiently. Although advisors have an obligation to provide a certain level of career information, their most important role is to teach students how to obtain, evaluate, and use it.

Sources for Collecting Occupational Information

There are many sources of career information and the ones students select will depend on the information they seek and the way they learn best. Some students might prefer searching for career information on the Internet, while others might benefit from talking with workers in the career fields they are exploring. Many of these information resources are described in Chapters 5 and 6. Students will find that using many sources is the most effective way to gather and compare information.

Internet Resources. The Internet has revolutionized access to career information. The sheer number of online listings has multiplied exponentially. Most professional societies, education institutions, business companies, and government agencies maintain Internet sites that provide information about many career-related topics.

O'Halloran, Fahr, and Keller (2002) caution Internet users to be aware of possible trouble with this ever changing resource. They used the guidelines of the National Career Development Association (NCDA) (1997) to guide their use of the Internet in career counseling. Although the Internet can be a useful tool for locating career information, at times its credibility, currency of information, and level of security might be questioned.

Since no one site can provide all the information needed, search engines such as Google or Yahoo! will help narrow down the sites after very specific topics are selected. Even then, an overwhelming number of sites for a particular topic can be displayed. For example, a search for *career interest inventories* yielded 142,000 hits. This is why career counselors' expertise is invaluable; they can help a student narrow down the Internet alternatives to a more targeted and manageable number.

Although many valuable career information Internet resources are provided by U.S. government agencies, there are many others that focus on more specific topics, such as Web sites for educational and professional organizations, state and local governments, and commercial sites (for example, test publishers). A particularly useful Web site for advisors is the NACADA National Clearinghouse (http://www.nacada.ksu.edu), which contains many topics relevant to career advising. (Chapters 5 and 6 provide more Internet sites, and Appendix A lists some useful career-advising Web sites as well.) Advisors will find it interesting to explore some of these resources by searching for the career fields associated with the academic discipline they advise and bookmarking those that are most relevant.

Print Resources. Libraries and career centers are important repositories of printed materials. Local, state, and federal government materials are also useful sources of printed career information. Professional societies, educational institutions, businesses, and trade associations are excellent sources of educational and occupational information. Some examples follow.

- The U.S. Department of Labor provides print materials about every facet of information related to occupations, worker traits, employment, projections of future labor force needs, and many other areas. Pamphlets and books are available free or for a nominal cost about many topics. One important resource is the *Occupational Outlook Quarterly (OOQ)*, a magazine that publishes the most recent labor market projections and articles about "Choosing Jobs," "Earnings and Benefits," "Education and Training," "Occupations and Industries," "Outlook and Trends," "Workers Without a Bachelor's

Degree," and "You're a What?" (descriptions of unusual occupations). The address for the online version of the *OOQ* is http://stats.bls.gov.

- Many organizations provide information about special populations, such as the disabled, older workers, women workers, as well as veterans. Directories are available in library reference centers. For example, state vocational rehabilitation agencies provide information for disabled workers about employment opportunities for people with many types of disabilities.

In addition to the Web site, a print version of the *Occupational Outlook Handbook 2004–2005* is published by the JIST Publishing Company (http://www.jist.com). The *O*NET Dictionary of Occupational Titles (DOT)* and the *Guide for Occupational Exploration* (Farr, Ludden, & Shatkin, 2001) are published in print form by the same publisher. Both may be obtained at any bookstore.

Many useful printed career materials are available in most libraries. The *Encyclopedia of Careers and Vocational Guidance* (2001), for example, is a four-volume reference to vocational information, including 2,500 job titles. It contains career articles, on-the-job interviews, industry information, and a list of career Web sites. A career guidance section provides information on interviewing and networking. Advisors need to visit the career services offices on their campuses to learn firsthand the types of printed information resources available to their advisees.

Other Information Sources. There are many other methods for collecting career information. Advisors may recommend that students interview workers in the career fields they are considering; volunteer in workplaces similar to those in which they have an interest; seek part-time or summer jobs in related workplaces; or obtain internships through their departments or career services on campus. Many campuses have established volunteer opportunities for students. Cooperative as well as internship experiences are available on many campuses. Any firsthand experience in a work environment will offer opportunities to gather information that other methods cannot duplicate. It is also known to be an excellent reference for employment later.

Evaluating Information

Advisors need to help students evaluate any career information they have gathered regardless of the source. A few questions for advisors and students to consider include:

- When was the information collected? Is it current or out of date? (Generally information more than two years old is probably no longer reliable.)
- What is the source of the information? Are the authors trying to sell you something, or is the information accurate and objective?
- How was the information collected? Is it from a reliable source (for example, U.S. government, state or local agencies)?

Advisors can help students separate good information from poor, fact from fiction. Students need to understand that information is just data until it is actually applied to and weighed in evaluating alternatives. One of the goals of career advising is to teach students where they can find career information and how to interpret it within the context of their place in the exploration process. Teaching students to evaluate the information they have collected for its accuracy, currency, and lack of bias is as important as teaching them how to collect it.

When collecting and evaluating information, advisors need to be aware of their own occupational stereotypes as well as those of their students (for example, the best prelaw major is political science; few men are in the nursing profession; accountants sit at computers all day). Stereotypes might limit exploring or seeking information about certain career fields or occupations because they (falsely) might seem inappropriate or inaccessible.

Summary

The INFORM phase of the career-advising process involves advisors in helping students find reliable sources of career information that are focused on their particular academic and career interests. Helping students search for career information can be challenging. Although the career resources on campus are the primary repository for this information, advisors must be conversant with the career-related information that is relevant to the academic disciplines for which they advise. Staying abreast of the latest and most accurate career information will increase their competence in helping students with academic decisions. In order to make good referrals, advisors should visit their institutions' career services offices so that they have firsthand knowledge of what is available. Actively involving themselves in Internet searches and other methods for collecting career information related to the academic programs they advise will greatly enhance their personal contacts with students and add an interesting dimension to their advising.

5

THE 3-I PROCESS

INTEGRATE

The INQUIRE and INFORM chapters have outlined advisor roles in clarifying student questions and helping them search for information that is vital to the career-planning process. In the INTEGRATE phase, advisors and students determine what additional assistance is needed to help students organize and make meaningful connections between the information sources they have collected. The term *integrate* is used in this context to mean coordinating or blending all the student knows into a functioning or unified whole. For example, students may need assistance with integrating:

- Self-information with academic major information
- Academic major information with occupational information
- Self-information with occupational information
- All the information they have collected together

This chapter describes some occupational classification systems that have been developed to organize massive amounts of educational and career information based on many different factors. These systems can help students make the connections between personal, academic area, and occupational information so that it can be integrated into a manageable form. The systems described include the the Standard Occupational Classification (SOC) System, *O*NET*, Holland's personal-environment system, and ACT's *World-of-Work Map*. While on the surface some of these systems may seem complicated, once learned they can make a significant difference in the ease with which many facets of personal and occupational exploration can be discovered and connected.

Other integrative influences are also addressed, including decision making and personal issues. When advisors are aware of personal characteristics other than interests and abilities that may affect the way students approach academic and career decision making, they may recognize personal issues such as career readiness and vocational identity that may facilitate or impede a student's progress.

It is ideal, of course, for a student to be able to work with one advisor over a period of time. Although one-stop contacts make dealing with career issues difficult, there are times when some students need to review what they know or rethink some earlier decisions. At key times, advisors may be the only individuals on campus who can help them generate these insights or help them change academic directions. At other times advisors need to reassure students that the paths they are on are good ones.

Career Classification Systems

The amount and complexity of career information makes it difficult for both advisors and students to find what they are looking for without using some of the systems that have been created to organize it into a variety of formats. These systems are also invaluable in helping pull together disparate bits of information into a cohesive, understandable whole. Many, especially the computer-assisted guidance systems, can help students integrate all the information necessary to make a decision. It is then up to the student to weigh and evaluate what he or she knows and use it to make a decision or solve a problem. The U.S. government systems are perhaps the best known, but there are other user-friendly systems that can help the searcher access information in a manageable, orderly way.

Occupational information is organized by theoretical frameworks, such as John Holland's (1997), as well as information systems, such as the U.S. Department of Labor's *O*NET*. Whether students are trying to access career information on their own or with the help of an advisor, they need to know the most efficient methods for mounting a search. One of the most powerful aspects of these systems is how they help students connect all the information they have collected into summaries the students can use in decision making. The systems can also help students integrate what they already know with the new information they have collected.

U.S. Government Systems

The U.S. Department of Labor (DOL) provides several systems for organizing career information.

Guide for Occupational Exploration (GOE). The GOE (Farr, Ludden, & Shatkin, 2001) is "a simple, commonsense way to explore career options based on [a student's] interests" (p. 1). The GOE is organized into fourteen major interest areas and 158 work groups that reflect the new economy. (The GOE areas are used in Chapter 4 to demonstrate how values may be connected with groups of occupations.) All job titles are organized within increasingly narrow job clusters that share many of the same work characteristics. For example, the first GOE career area—Arts, Entertainment, and Media—is given the code number 01. More specific occupations within this career area are organized into ten work groups. Writers and editors, for example, fall under 01.02 Writing and Editing. Sports: Coaching, Instructing, Officiating and Performing is assigned to the last code, 01.10. Specific jobs within the work groups are given two additional numbers. For example, Fitness Trainers and Aerobics Instructors are under 01.10.01. Since each occupation is given a GOE code, these numbers can be used to cross-reference other occupational systems that use the same code.

Standard Occupational Classification (SOC) System. Although advisors will probably not use this system directly, they should be aware that it is used by all federal agencies collecting information so that all occupational data can be compared. The SOC system (http://stats.bls.gov/soc) classifies workers across four levels from twenty-three major groups to 821 detailed occupations. This system is flexible enough to assimilate new occupations as they become known, which has been a problem with other systems in the past.

One of the most useful resources that bases its occupational descriptions on the SOC system is the *Occupational Outlook Handbook (OOH)*. The OOH offers descriptions of the occupations in the United States that represent 88 percent of all the jobs in the U.S. economy. Its information is compiled every two years by the U.S. Department of Labor. Included for each occupation are the nature of the work, working conditions, employment, job outlook, training and education needed, earnings, related occupations, and additional information sources, including Web sites. Other practical sections feature sources of career information, finding a job and evaluating a job offer, and projections of the labor force and occupation and industry employment for the next ten-year period.

O*NET. Since 1939, the U.S. government has provided the definitive description of all the jobs in the United States. *O*NET* is its new, comprehensive, automated replacement (http://www.onetcenter.org). Compiled by the Bureau of Labor Statistics, it contains the most accurate and updated information about more than 950 occupations that are key to the U.S. economy. It is also organized according to the SOC system.

Students can use *O*NET* to find occupations to explore, search for occupations that use designated skills, view occupation summaries and details, use crosswalks from other classification systems to find corresponding *O*NET* occupations, view related occupations, create and print customized reports outlining their search results, and link to other online information resources.

An *O*NET* tool that students will find particularly useful is a "snapshot" of an occupation that summarizes information about its important aspects (www.online.onetcenter.org). The snapshot includes experience requirements, worker requirements, worker characteristics, occupation requirements, occupation-specific information, and occupation characteristics. A "details" section provides the level of importance for each of eight areas for selected occupations, including knowledge, skills, abilities, interests, work values, work context, tasks, and work activities. O*NET information links directly to other labor market information, such as wage and employment statistics.

O*NET uses the U.S. Department of Labor's Standard Occupation Classification (SOC) to organize occupation descriptions, tasks, information about related occupations, occupational families, and detailed work activities. The O*NET link to occupational information for the disabled is http://online.onetcenter.org/help/links/#Accom.

The O*NET Career Exploration Tools are a set of career exploration and assessment tools that help students identify their work-related interests and abilities and what they consider important on the job. They can then explore occupations that match their interests, abilities, and preferences. The Career Exploration Tools include (1) O*NET® Interest Profiler™; (2) O*NET® Work Importance Locator and Work Importance Profiler™; and (3) O*NET® Ability Profiler™.

Holland's Person-Environment System

Another widely used system is based on John Holland's theoretical framework, described in Chapter 2. Holland characterizes people by their resemblance to six personality types: Realistic, Investigative, Artistic, Social, Enterprising, and Conventional (RIASEC). "The more closely a person resembles a particular type, the more likely he or she is to exhibit the personal traits and behaviors associated with that type" (Holland, 1997, p. 1). Holland then characterizes the environments in which people live and work as six model environments with the same names (RIASEC). When people and work environments are paired, certain outcomes can be predicted. "These outcomes include vocational choice, vocational stability and achievement, educational choice and achievement, personal competence, social behavior, and susceptibility to influence" (p. 2). Holland indicates that people search for work environments that suit their skills, abilities, attitudes, and values. An Enterprising personality, for example, will seek an Enterprising work environment, such as marketing, public relations, or law. Since people reflect more than one type of personality, Holland assigns a three-letter code to represent a person's dominant types. For example, CRS describes a person whose most dominant type is Conventional, then Realistic and then Social. Work environments also display dominant characteristics and are also assigned three-letter codes. Accountants, for example, are assigned a CRS code. Holland suggests that when CRS personalities work in CRS environments, they will probably be satisfied with their work, since their skills, abilities, attitudes, and values match those of the work tasks that accountants perform. (This description of Holland's theory is an oversimplification. For a more detailed explanation, consult his book, *Making Vocational Choices*, 1997.)

Applications of Holland's theory are useful in organizing educational as well as occupational information since the theory describes both people and the environments they prefer. Smart, Feldman, and Ethington (2000) classified academic disciplines in terms of Holland's types. They found that the Realistic and Conventional disciplines were difficult to classify since there were such small numbers of college faculty members and students in these disciplines. They found that the number of students in the Investigative and Artistic environments reflected small changes and those in the Enterprising environment remained stable. The largest change among students in all of the Holland environments, however, was among those in the Social environment. Smart et al. concluded that "faculty create academic environments inclined to require, reinforce, and reward the distinctive patterns of abilities and interests of students in a manner consistent with Holland's theory" (p. 96) and that "faculty members in different clusters of academic disciplines create distinctly different academic environments" (p. 238). Smart et al. offer the interesting idea of reorganizing academic departments by RIASEC type. This would provide a connection between faculty in fields who share the same Holland environment but are separated by traditional departmental organization.

Some career libraries have organized their holdings around Holland's types; many interest inventories provide Holland types in relation to interest areas; the computer-assisted career guidance program *DISCOVER* uses Holland's system to help organize its *World-of-Work Map* (see next section); and many career and advising offices generate lists of their majors by Holland types. This method for organizing career information is an excellent way to help students connect their personal characteristics with educational and occupational fields and can help them narrow their focus of academic and career exploration.

World-of-Work Map

ACT's *World-of-Work Map* is based on the degree that occupations work with data, people, things, and ideas. The map is organized around six occupational clusters: Administrative and Sales, Business Operations, Technical, Science and Technology, Arts, and Social Service. Job Family Charts (ACT, 2001) plot more than 500 occupations on the map. College majors can also be plotted using this system.

The organizing systems students use will depend on the information resource and the type of information they are seeking. *O*NET*, for example, uses the Department of Labor's SOC system; the *World-of-Work Map* uses Holland's system. Three of these systems are described in Table 5.1 by the way they classify or organize thousands of occupations. Although the systems use different methods and titles, they are similar in the way they group occupations

Table 5.1   Occupational Classification Systems

GOE Codes	Holland Codes	World-of-Work Map
01 Arts, Entertainment, and Media	Artistic Social	T. Applied Arts (Visual) U. Creative & Performing Arts V. Applied Arts (Written and Spoken)
02 Science, Math, and Engineering	Investigative Realistic	O. Engineering and Technologies P. Natural Sciences & Technologies J. Computer/Info Specialties
03 Plants and Animals	Investigative Realistic	P. Natural Sciences & Technologies I. Ag/Forestry & Related
04 Law, Law Enforcement, and Public Safety	Investigative Realistic Enterprising	D. Regulation & Protection
05 Mechanics, Installers, and Repairers	Realistic Conventional	N. Mechanical & Electrical Specialties
06 Construction, Mining, and Drilling	Realistic Conventional	K. Construction & Maintenance
07 Transportation	Realistic Enterprising Conventional	H. Transport Operation & Related

according to work tasks and worker characteristics. They also integrate other information into their systems so that there are connections to personal characteristics and academic majors.

Decision Making: The Heart of the Integrative Process

A problem for some students during the INTEGRATE phase is the very nature and complexity of career decision making. Decision making is a complicated process and involves very personal think-

Table 5.1 (*continued*)

GOE Codes	Holland Codes	World-of-Work Map
08 Industrial Production	Realistic	M. Manufacturing & Processing L. Crafts & Related
09 Business Detail	Conventional Enterprising	E. Communications & Records F. Financial Transactions G. Distribution & Dispatching
10 Sales and Marketing	Enterprising Realistic Conventional	A. Employment-Related Services B. Marketing & Sales C. Management
11 Recreation, Travel, and Other Personal Services	Enterprising Realistic	Z. Personal Services
12 Education and Social Service	Social Enterprising	X. Education Y. Community Services S. Social Sciences
13 General Management and Support	Enterprising Conventional Social	C. Management F. Financial Transactions
14 Medical and Health Services	Investigative Social Artistic	Q. Medical Technologies R. Medical Diagnosis & Treatment W. Health Care

ing patterns and behaviors. Advisors need to be aware of the different elements involved and how students differ in the way they approach it.

Decision-Making Styles

Students have their own unique ways of making decisions. Dinklage (1968) was one of the first to identify different styles, and she described eight (for example, delaying, impulsive, compliant, intuitive). She suggested that the "planful" style led to a greater probability of making an informed choice. Satisfying decisions can also be made when intuition is used along with planfulness.

Understanding their decision-making styles can help students integrate their personal approaches into general knowledge about the decision-making process. It can also help them understand how some of the decision-making habits they have formed can help or hinder the effectiveness of the process as they move through it. For example, deciding between two or three coats in a store does not require as much thought and information as choosing a major. A slower, more systematic approach might be warranted in the latter situation. Two examples of how styles can be determined follow.

Decision-Making Inventory (DMI). Coscarelli (1983) developed a decision-making style assessment that measures two important factors in making decisions: *how* information is processed and *where* the information is processed. The *how* ranges from systematic to spontaneous and the *where* from internal (thinking) to external (talking). A spontaneous person makes a quick, intuitive decision and later tests it against information. A systematic person feels more comfortable gathering a lot of information before making a decision. Once the information has been gathered, the external decision maker likes to *talk* about it with others. The internal decision maker needs to *think* about the information before talking to anyone about it. When the two dimensions of information gathering and analyzing are combined, four distinct decision-making styles can be identified: spontaneous internal, spontaneous external, systematic internal, and systematic external. Although no one fits into any of these styles completely, thinking about why they feel comfortable making decisions one way over another can offer insights into how they gather and process information (Sears & Gordon, 2002).

Learning Style Inventory (LSI). The LSI is based on the work of David Kolb (1967), who created an experiential learning model. Although not a decision-making style instrument, it can be used to identify different ways students learn the decision-making process.

The model consists of four elements: (1) concrete experience, (2) observation and reflection, (3) the formation of abstract concepts, and (4) testing in new situations or action. Kolb represented these four learning styles by an experiential learning circle. Learners can begin at any of the four points in the cycle, but Kolb suggests that the learning process is really a spiral. Learning entails the possession of four different abilities, which are placed at one of the poles of each dimension. These abilities are concrete experience, reflective observations, abstract conceptualization, and active experimentation.

Kolb's learning styles include the *Converger*, who is strong in practical applications of ideas, employs deductive reasoning, and has narrow interests. The *Diverger* is imaginative, good at seeing things from different perspectives, is people oriented, and has broad cultural interests. The *Assimilator* is strong at creating theoretical models, excels in inductive reasoning, and is more concerned with abstract concepts than people, while the *Accommodator's* greatest strengths are in doing things, solving problems intuitively, is a risk taker, and performs well when required to react to immediate circumstances (Kolb, 1981). The Learning Style Inventory was developed to measure these different learning approaches. When applied to career advising, it can demonstrate how students learn through concrete experiences, taking time to reflect and conceptualize what they are learning, and then actively experimenting with their choice, such as selecting certain coursework or engaging in an internship experience. Kolb's experiential learning model indicates how students approach learning activities, including decision making from many different perspectives.

Brain Processes

Another way to consider how students approach decision making is to consider the hemispheric differences in the brain and how they affect thinking and learning. Each hemisphere has different traits: left-brain traits include language, logic, numbers, sequence, linear, symbolic representation, judgmental. Right-brain traits include images, rhythm, music, imagination, color, patterns, emotions, nonjudgmental (Wycoff, 1991). The left side of the brain processes information in a linear, sequential manner from the parts to the whole. The right side processes from the whole to the parts. It sees the big picture. The left-brain person learns in sequence and can process symbols such as letters, words, and math symbols efficiently. The right-brain person is more concrete and wants to see, feel, and touch things.

The left and right hemispheres process information in different ways in problem solving and decision making. Most people have a dominant side, but the learning and thinking process is enhanced when both sides participate in a balanced way.

Taking Action

A decision is never final until action is taken to implement it. Advisors need to help students develop an action plan that includes the steps necessary to implement the decision along with a timeline for completing it. For example, a student who is changing majors might need to file the institutional paperwork, redo their course schedule, meet with a new advisor, and look into the extracurricular and other opportunities the new major offers (for example, internships, student clubs).

Most students do not approach problems systematically and need to learn the process. Advisors can often tell when students are moving in the right direction or if they need to be guided to explore other options. Advisors also need to be aware of how they personally approach decision making so they are more aware of why they may be having difficulty communicating with a student who is approaching the process from an entirely different perspective. Implementing a decision is an important part of the integrative phase.

Other Academic and Career Choice Influences

There may be times during the INTEGRATE phase when advisors sense some students are struggling with other issues affecting or preventing them from making an academic or career-related decision.

Many factors influence how individuals choose a career, prepare for it, enter it, succeed in the work, and enjoy satisfaction from it. Some important factors that may be influencing students' decision-making ability are family, socioeconomic status, gender, ethnicity, and physical status, to name a few.

Sociological studies offer insights into the impact that work has on individuals and their lives. Some examples discussed by Brown (2002) include occupational prestige and mobility, admissions requirements for some occupations (for example, licensing, certification), and regulations that control worker behavior.

Economic conditions and changes, such as supply and demand, employment and unemployment, and how change affects the structure of work, can also influence career choices. First-year college students, for example, who choose certain career fields because they are considered "hot jobs" at that time may find that upon graduation technological changes have greatly altered the field and there is no longer a need for large numbers of workers.

Personal Influences

Personal factors influence students' career-seeking attitudes and behaviors and suggest the type of career-related assistance they need. Although some of these are obviously beyond the scope of advising assistance, advisors need to be aware that there are many personal issues that affect how students make academic and career decisions. A few of these factors found in the career and psychological literature are described next.

Vocational Self-Concept. Self-concept may be described as how individuals picture themselves in a work situation or position. Career decisions reflect attempts at translating self-understanding (that is, self-concepts) into career terms (Super & Bohn, 1970). According to Super, individuals' self-concepts, or their "pictures of themselves, influences their actions and helps determine the occupations they prefer, the kind of training they undertake, and the degree of satisfaction they experience on the job" (p. 108).

Self-understanding is obtained by comparing one's self objectively to others. How one's uniqueness is focused, however, is subjective. These insights help people form and set appropriate career goals (Niles & Harris-Bowlsbey, 2002).

Advisors might ask students to picture themselves in certain work settings. What do they like in this work situation? What don't they like about this work? Some decided students who can adequately describe themselves in their chosen work environments may have based their descriptions on solid knowledge and experience. Other decided students may have difficulty picturing themselves in a workplace since they lack information about what is involved in the work tasks and other work-related attributes. Still other students may base their answers on stereotypical impressions. Students who need more information can be encouraged to take part in assessment (for example, testing, computer-assisted programs), interviewing workers in the field, volunteering, or in other hands-on exploration activities.

Indecisiveness. Some students enter college undecided about an academic or career direction. For most students this is a natural, developmentally sound choice. There are a few students, however, who have difficulty making any decision, including those associated with everyday life. Many years ago Tyler (1953) identified these differences between students who are *undecided* and those who are *indecisive*. Indecisiveness is a result of unsatisfactory habits or thinking that permeates the individual's total life. Until these personal problems or uncertainties can be resolved, a career or educational decision cannot be made. Advisors should refer to counseling those few students who can't make a commitment to any academic or career direction and who display high levels of anxiety. It is important to recognize that these few students need counseling help beyond the expertise of academic advisors (Gordon, 1995).

Self-Efficacy. Self-efficacy refers to individuals' judgments of their own capabilities to perform a given task or behavior. Those who judge themselves capable of performing certain tasks or activities will engage in them; those who believe the tasks are beyond their capabilities will avoid them. This concept is especially helpful to advisors when observing a student's career decision-making behavior (Betz, 2004; Betz & Hackett, 1986). Students who avoid majors that require high-level math courses might have low self-efficacy in that content area, for example. Self-efficacy is also involved in how confident students are in performing the tasks associated with making career decisions. For example, students who have complete confidence in their ability to choose a major or career that will fit their interests have high self-efficacy in that task.

A study by Taylor and Popma (1990) found that an instrument measuring career self-efficacy was able to differentiate three groups of students categorized on the basis of college major status: declared majors, those with tentative major choices, and undecided students. As advisors work with students who are having difficulty making major or career decisions, they can ask the students to identify the tasks they think are involved and how they judge their ability to perform those tasks. Self-efficacy is sometimes associated with career maturity.

Career Maturity. Many advisors have been in contact with students who don't seem motivated or ready to take part in any activities related to academic and/or career planning. Some students may be "career immature," that is, they are not ready to make educational and occupational decisions. Career maturity is based on an individual's readiness to engage in or cope with the normal developmental tasks associated with career exploration, planning, and decision making (Super, 1990). According to Super, traditional-age college students who are in the exploratory stage will want to make plans for career development, explore occupations, and will want to know how to make career decisions. Super uses the term *adaptability* when referring to adult students who are able to handle changing career situations or goals.

Peterson, Lenz, and Sampson (2003) discuss readiness in terms of students' "ability to successfully engage in academic programs and to use student services in ways that enhance learning within a social context" (p. 105). Advisors may find that a few students, especially first-year students, may not be ready to deal with all the changes that come with adjustment and academic and career decision making. Although advisors may feel some frustration with certain students who seem to be delaying their involvement in these tasks, eventually most will engage in them in their own time or because of institutional demands.

Integrative Questions

Example of questions that advisors might ask based on the information systems and decision-making influences outlined above include:

- What information was used in making a decision?
- What (if any) information is still needed?
- What conclusions has the student drawn from this information?
- What doubts (if any) does the student still have?
- Are they still uncomfortable about anything?
- Are they ready to make a decision or have they already made one?
- What do they like about their decision?
- What do they need to do next?

When students are ready to delve into the career decision-making process, they are aware that they need to take an active part in the various activities associated with it. Advisors can act as a stimulus for this activity by taking away the mystery of what questions to ask, how to gather the pertinent information, and how to make sense of what they have learned along the way.

Summary

The 3-I Process is not intended as a literal explanation of how to approach students with career-advising problems. Most advisors use their own effective version of this process. Advisors need to determine where students are in their readiness and commitment to career exploration, what information about their personal strengths and limitations they possess and what they still need to gather, and what help they need to integrate what they know so that a decision can be made. Helping students take the actions necessary to bring closure to a decision is an important final step. Figure 5.1 summarizes the different factors that are at play in the

Figure 5.1 Factors in the Integrative Process

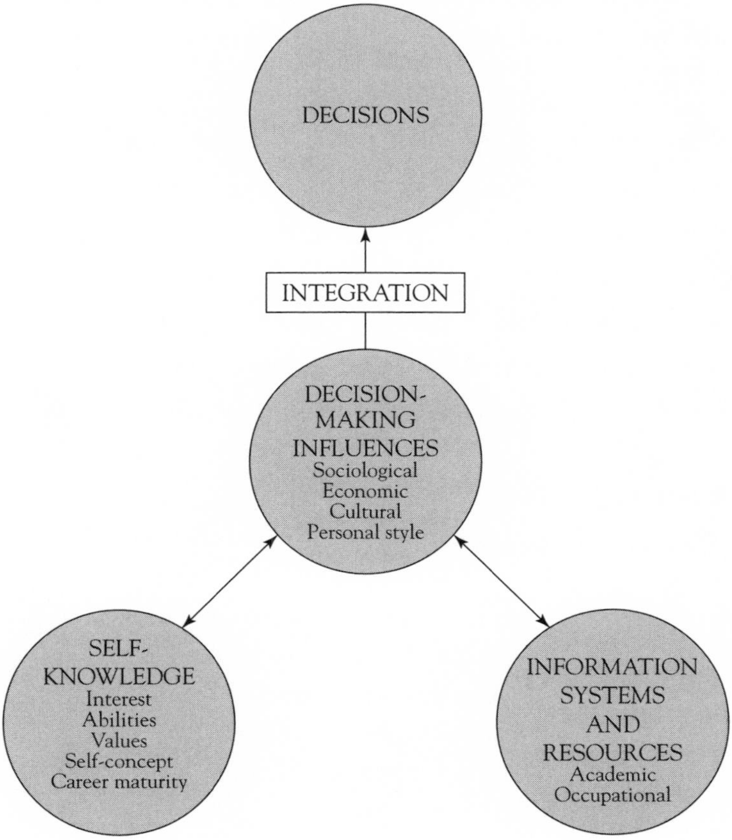

academic/career decision-making and problem-solving integrative process.

All students bring a unique set of perceptions and possible solutions to their own problems. It is up to the advisor and student together to determine what personal and environmental factors are involved in the problems and identify the best approaches for resolving them. The next chapter describes various methods and resources that can assist advisors as the need for career advising evolves.

6

CAREER-ADVISING RESOURCES

As indicated previously, career information and advice should be integrated naturally into regular advising sessions. Although many of the methods and techniques required in career advising are the same as those used in academic advising, the nature of the questions and information resources are often different. The organizational systems described in Chapter 5 offer vehicles for accessing some of these resources. Other approaches and their applications are described following.

The resources that advisors use to provide career information and career-planning assistance will depend on the student's concerns, the advisor's expertise and experience with various resources, and the time allotted for the advising contact. Some students prefer a more structured, computer-assisted way of gathering information, while others benefit from interviewing workers in the careers that interest them. The advisor's and student's perceptions of the nature of the problem or need will determine which resources are suggested. The career-advising resources described in this chapter are group advising, career courses, computerized career guidance programs, Internet resources, and assessment. Although many students consider individual advising the most desirable, other ways of delivering career information and assistance are just as effective, depending on where the student is in the academic and career decision-making process.

Group Career Advising

Advising students in groups has several advantages. Larger numbers of students can be served and advisors' time can be maximized. Research has confirmed that structured career-planning interventions have a positive effect on college students' career development (Crites, 1981; Kivlighan, 1990; Krumboltz, 1996). Some students benefit from hearing other students express concerns similar to their own. Many career-advising groups are structured to offer information that can be used to supplement what advisors discuss in one-to-one sessions. Some examples of group advising include:

- Workshops in which a specific topic is covered (for example, "What can I do with a major in [*occupation title*]?")
- Hands-on career information searches that take place in a career library
- Interpretation of inventories and other career-related instruments, such as the Self-Directed Search (SDS) or the Harrington-O'Shea Career Decision Making System (CDMS) (described later in this chapter)
- Workshops for major-changers who have been denied admission to a selective admissions major
- Departmental workshops for seniors who want to learn job search skills

The purpose of the group advising session should be clearly communicated to the students, and they should be informed at the outset what will be involved. Students who take part in career-advising groups (1) learn from other students with similar concerns, (2) acquire new information about academic and career relationships, and (3) learn more in-depth information about themselves and different academic and career options. Another benefit for some students is the emotional and social support they receive from their peers.

Advisors who conduct workshops on career topics should have the expertise to address students' career-related needs. Some of the most useful and effective career-oriented group sessions or workshops are designed and carried out by academic advisors and career counselors working together. Students' questions and problems are thus addressed from both academic and career perspectives.

The career topics suitable for group interventions are limitless. Sessions can be of varying duration, one-hour, several in sequence, or over a college term. Group advising sessions can be efficient vehicles for enhancing the integration of academic and career-advising information.

Career Courses

Another vehicle for meeting the career needs of groups of students is the academic course that incorporates self-assessment, the exploration of educational and occupational information, and decision making. Career courses, like freshman seminars, can be traced back to the early 1900s (Vernick, Reardon, & Sampson, 2002). Many studies of career courses have found that students who participated in them made more realistic decisions, developed greater self-awareness, reduced negative career thoughts, better understood the realities of the job market, and increased career decidedness (Brooks, 1995; Hardesty, 1991; Reed, Reardon, Lenz, & Leierer, 2001). Bluestein (1992) suggests that career courses can improve students' competence in self- and occupational exploration and can serve as a means for modeling appropriate decision-making behavior.

In a recent e-mail survey of career services by Halasz and Kempton (2000), more than two-thirds of the forty institutions that responded indicated they offered a career course. Course content was classified as dealing with career decision making, career exploration, and job search skills and strategies.

Courses with an academic major focus have proved to be effective in providing much-needed information on career and graduate study options in an organized and systematic way (Dodson, Chastain, & Landrum, 1996). An example of a course that specifically emphasizes academic major exploration and decision making involves students in *taking stock* (of where they are in the academic decision-making process); *exploring self* (exercises in assessing interests, aptitudes, skills, and values); *exploring academic majors* (from three different approaches); *exploring occupations* (general career fields and hands-on information gathering); and *decision making* (experiencing the process, integrating academic and occupational information, making and implementing a decision, setting goals) (Gordon & Sears, 2004). When career courses are based on both academic and career exploration and choice, students learn that majors don't always lead to a specific occupation and that many majors can prepare them for successful careers.

Books that are used as course texts emphasize career planning and decision making. A few examples are *Turning Points: Your Career Decision-Making Guide* by Diane Ducat (2002); *Making Career Decisions That Count: A Practical Guide* by Darrell Luzzo (2002); and *Connect College to Career: Student Guide to Work and Life Transition* by P. Hettich (2005). The first two books, and Gordon and Sears (2004), are practical guides for helping students make effective academic and career decisions. The third book concentrates on helping upper-class students prepare for the workplace.

A popular version of the career course is taught by some institutions as part of their distance learning program. These are sometimes used as "entry" courses or as first-time distance courses, especially for adults who are in a career transition or want to try out a practical course that gives them a distance experience.

Whiston, Sexton, and Lasoff (1998) found that next to individual and group counseling, career courses were more effective than any other career intervention, such as workshops or computer interventions. Advisors should consider a referral to this option when working with students who need a longer-term, structured approach to academic and career exploration.

Computerized Career Guidance Programs

When an advisor refers a student to the campus career services office or library, the student may be introduced to a computer program that provides a system for organized career exploration. These systems have become extremely sophisticated after many years of development, and most are very user-friendly. The interactive programs they provide assist students in gathering self-, educational, and occupational information and help them integrate this information into decision making and planning. The advantage of a computer-assisted program over printed materials is that the computer materials are frequently updated and therefore provide more current information.

Niles and Harris-Bowlsbey (2002) list some of the strengths of computer-assisted systems. They can administer and interpret tests and inventories; search large databases; monitor the progress of the user through the career-planning process; deliver interactive instruction; and link students to other resources, such as Web sites for further information (pp. 212–213). The authors warn, however, that computer-assisted systems should not be used without human support services. Some students may not be ready to receive information from a computer, need interpretation of tests and inventories, need help with identifying personal values, and need motivational and emotional support for continuing their career planning.

Iaccarino (2002) provides an extensive list of computer-assisted systems and offers an overview of their unique features (pp. 176–181). A few are described following. Two of the earliest systems were the System of Interactive Guidance Information (SIGI) (http://www.valparint.com) and *DISCOVER* (http://www.act.org/discover). These two systems are still very much in use today.

SIGI Plus. The software for *SIGI Plus* integrates self-assessment with career information that helps students view realistically the best educational and career options for their future success. As students work through *SIGI Plus*, they can clarify their work-related values; create a list of occupations based on their values, interests, and work skills; create a list of occupations based on college major fields of study; obtain up-to-date information and printouts on hundreds of occupations; determine education and training requirements for each occupation; and put their career plans into action.

DISCOVER. *DISCOVER* also involves students in self-assessment and educational and occupational exploration. Like *SIGI Plus*, *DISCOVER* takes students through various modules involving self-assessment, learning about occupations, making educational choices, and future planning. It assists students in acquiring the skills needed for job preparation, résumé writing, cover letters, and interviewing. *DISCOVER* also contains a module on transitions that might be particularly helpful to older adult students. Internet links are also provided.

ACT, Inc., has recently revised the descriptions of majors in *DISCOVER*, using the revised Classification Instruction Programs (CIP) list from the U.S. National Center for Education Statistics (NCES) (2002) (nces.ed.gov/pubsearch). *DISCOVER* offers full descriptions for 444 majors. Each major's description includes the purpose of the major; characteristics necessary to succeed in it; typical college courses; links to related occupations; specialties within this major; and links to related majors. This information is extremely helpful to students who are undecided or who are changing majors.

Focus II. *Focus II* (http://www. focuscareer.com) involves students in self-assessment; explores and analyzes occupational and educational paths compatible with their personal attributes; helps students set goals; and identifies training and developmental needs. Students progress through the program in seven phases. *Focus II* helps students examine occupations based on educational areas of studies, education level, and the skills and training required.

Choices CT. *Choices CT* (http://www.bridges.com/usa/product/ choices) is geared to adults in career transition, offers interest and skills inventories, and relates their transferable skills, interests, and priorities to educational and career alternatives. An electronic port-folio helps students organize information about themselves, and interactive modules help them focus on job search skills.

The Career Information Delivery Systems Inventory (Olson & Whitman, 1990) highlights the similarities and differences across nineteen computerized career information delivery systems so that practitioners can make more informed choices when considering what system to adopt. Whatever system students use, its effective-ness will depend on where they are in the academic and career decision-making process, their readiness to take part, and what type of information they need. A review of studies by Iaccarino (2002) did not find any program more effective than another. He found the main reason career services selected a particular system was usually its cost.

Internet Resources

As indicated in Chapters 4 and 5, the Internet has become an important tool for providing a variety of methods for career infor-mation and exploration. There are thousands of resources on the Internet for career decision making, including career assessment inventories and all facets of the career decision-making process itself. Students trying to access these resources without some guid-ance, however, may be overwhelmed. Advisors and career services office should generate lists of Web sites that are relevant to the spe-cific needs of their students. They can help students initiate searches in their office, give them "homework," and follow up later. Boer (2001), for example, lists more than 130 career-related Web sites that she uses in her online career counseling practice.

As described in Chapter 5, *O*NET* is the U.S. Department of Labor's online information network. An additional resource is the

Skills Search function (http://online.onetcenter.org/help/online/skills), which can help students use their skills to identify occupations for exploration. Students select skills from one or more of the six skill groups that they have or plan to acquire: Basic Skills, Complex Problem-Solving Skills, Resource Management Skills, Social Skills, Systems Skills, and Technical Skills. Student A selects the following skills from the six groups: mathematics, reading comprehension, and troubleshooting. After completing his choices, a table of occupations and the degree to which the skill matches is provided. In his case, chemical equipment controllers, office machine services, and respiratory therapy technician are a few of the occupations that match the skills he entered. He can then research these occupations in more detail through this system.

Resources on the Internet, however, must continually be updated, since many Web addresses change frequently or disappear. Like any educational or career-planning tool, the Internet is only one of many resources that should be used in helping students with career exploration and planning.

Some additional Web sites to which advisors might refer students are described following.

MyRoad.com. MyRoad.com is the College Board's career planning Web site. It covers six areas: Insights, I.D.Me, Explore Majors, Find a College, Research Careers, and My Plan. Students can take a personality assessment, explore majors (majors are divided into six fields: engineering, humanities, interdisciplinary studies, life sciences, physical sciences, and social sciences) and careers (450 are described), and create an online portfolio for career planning. Institutional and individual subscriptions are available.

CareerScope. This program (http://www.vri.org) contains self-administered tests that measure both aptitudes and interests and matches high aptitudes with high interest areas. Opportunities for further occupational research are provided.

The Keirsey Character Sorter. This personality inventory (http://www.keirsey.com) uncovers individuals' innate tendencies, preferences, and motivations that reveal an integrated view of their personalities.

The Career Key. The Career Key (http://www.careerkey.org) was developed by Lawrence Jones at North Carolina State University. It allows students to assess their interests, values, abilities, and skills; compare these attributes to occupations they are considering; and find occupational descriptions through a link to the *Occupational Outlook Handbook*.

America's Career Information Network. This site (http://www.acinet.org) offers a way for students to assess their skills and then helps them match their skills to specific occupations.

Portfolio Development. Many institutions have developed their own Web sites that allow their students to keep track of their coursework, accomplishments, and other personal information that can be used for résumé and employment purposes. Some of these are used in conjunction with a career course (Vernick, Reardon, & Sampson, 2002). A well-known example is Florida State University's Career Portfolio Program, which helps students integrate curricular and cocurricular experiences (for example, academic/career advising, courses, and service learning) through an Internet-based system that promotes student learning, career preparation, and employment. One goal of the program is to positively support student recruitment and retention (Reardon, Lumsden, & Meyer, 2004).

CareerWAYS. CareerWAYS is an example of a for-fee computerized portfolio and planning system that helps users record and retrieve important personal data that can help in planning and making decisions. It transforms data into information students can use to develop class plans, résumés, and career and educational goals statements (http://www.innovativeeducation.com/cdsways/career_WAYS/career_ways.html).

Compared to other areas of career assessment, the Internet is still developing, and students need to be aware of the lack of research and experience with its many offerings. Students may be overwhelmed with the sheer number of career-related Web sites that Google or other search engines produce when *career planning* is used as a search term. With the help of an advisor or counselor, students should be able to narrow down and prioritize their searches so that the method for exploring responds directly to the type of assistance they need. Students and advisors should always remember that the Internet is not a secure environment. Confidentiality is always at risk even though a Web site has policies and methods in place to ensure privacy.

Assessment

Although academic advisors are not trained or expected to administer career assessments, it is sometimes helpful to be aware of some commonly used career-related tests and inventories. A few instruments are briefly described next. If advisors wish to become more familiar with career inventories and other assessment tools, they can visit the Web site of the ERIC Center for Assessment in Education at http://www.searcheric.org, or The Mental Measurements Yearbook (Tests in Print) at http://www.unl.edu/buros.

Self-Directed Search (SDS). John Holland's (1997) person-environment system is described in detail in Chapter 5. The Self-Directed Search is designed to measure Holland's six personality and six environmental types. It identifies a person's particular activities, competencies, and self-estimates compared with certain occupational groups. (A more detailed description of Holland's theory is provided in Chapters 2 and 5.)

Harrington-O'Shea Career Decision Making System *(CDMS)*. The CDMS (Harrington & O'Shea, 2003) is an interest inventory that provides an assessment of career interests, job choices, school subjects, future plans, values, and abilities. These attributes are then related to career clusters.

Career Thoughts Inventory (CTI). The CTI (Sampson, Peterson, Lenz, Reardon, & Saunders, 1996) helps individuals identify the career thoughts that may influence their career goals. Irrational career beliefs are known to affect the career decision-making process.

WorkKeys. *WorkKeys* measures skills in eleven areas: Reading for Information, Applied Mathematics, Listening, Writing, Locating Information, Applied Technology, Teamwork, Motivation, Learning, Observing, and Speaking. Specific jobs are profiled with the skills so that the student's skills can be related to the level required by specific occupations and jobs.

StrengthQuest. *StrengthQuest* (http://www.strengthquest.com) (Buckingham & Clifton, 2001) is a program that helps students become aware of their personal strengths. An online assessment tool reveals students' five greatest areas of talents or themes. A workbook and a Web site teach students how to build strengths and how to apply their talents and strengths in their academic work, careers, and lives.

Career Decision Scale (CDS). The CDS (Osipow, Carney, Winer, Yanico, & Koschier, 1997) provides an estimate of indecision about major and career and the reasons for being unable to make a vocational choice.

Card Sort. Although not an inventory, the card sort technique can be used in the same way. The card sort, as the name implies, is a deck of cards on which an occupation (or academic major or interest area) is written on one side of a card and a description of the occupation (or major or interest) on the other. Students are asked to sort the deck into three piles: occupations they would consider, those they absolutely would not consider, and those they have no feeling about one way or the other. Each occupation in the "would consider" pile is discussed by the advisor and student, and those that create the strongest interest are explored further. The student might look at the "ambivalent" pile for other occupations that he or she might want to switch to the "would consider" pile.

Discussing the "would not consider" pile, or what the student dislikes, can also generate valuable insights into the student's thinking. Students who have no choices or too many choices benefit from this exercise, since it forces them to choose between many alternatives and they can learn more about them as they sort. Card sort decks can be purchased commercially, or advisors can create their own decks of cards using whatever topics they wish to discuss with students (for example, their college's majors, work values).

Additional Inventories

Many other inventories are offered in campus career counseling and placement centers, including interest inventories (for example, the Strong Interest Inventory [SII], Kuder Occupational Interest Survey [KOIS], Career Occupational Preference Survey [COPS]); aptitude tests (for example, the General Aptitude Test Battery [GATB], developed by the U.S. Employment Service); and personality inventories. The Myers-Briggs Type Indicator (MBTI) is a commonly used test to measure psychological types that are based on Jungian theory. Using Myers-Briggs, students are able to relate their personality profile to groups of people who work in specific occupations. For more detailed information, visit the Web site at http://www.capt.org. Many of the inventories just mentioned are available online as well.

Advisors' Role

The career-advising resources described may serve as a resource for academic advisors who want to challenge their advisees in both academic and career exploration and planning. As indicated before, it is not the advisor's role to become a "career counselor," but to be knowledgeable about how students develop vocationally. They will be able to recognize career-related problems, expressed or not expressed by students, and help them take the appropriate steps to resolve them. Jurgens (2000) found that brief interventions were just as effective as long term in increasing career certainty and student satisfaction. Any advisor discussions about career-related topics, however brief, may have a positive effect on students' career thoughts.

As advisors work with their advisees on career-related problems, they can play an important role in referring them to other effective career resources. To make the most informed referrals, advisors need to educate themselves about career development, information, methods, and resources. Advisor development programs on career-related topics can be an important vehicle for acquiring these essential career knowledge areas and skills.

Some examples of other ways advisors might become involved in career advising include:

- Serving as an academic resource to a career-planning course, teaching the classes that relate to academic planning
- Developing a career-advising group of students who need additional help with academic and career exploration (for example, undecided students, major-changers)
- Working with a career counselor in developing workshops that provide academic and career-related information
- Visiting the career services on campus to which they might refer students so that they know firsthand what the students experience

- Participating in the computer-assisted systems on campus to become familiar with what their advisees will experience when referred to them

- Encouraging departmental academic advisors to meet with a group of campus career services providers on a regular basis to share information

- Spending some time on the Internet with career-related Web sites to become familiar with what students may find in their searches

- Developing a list of Web sites that are relevant to their academic areas of expertise and updating it frequently

- Developing handouts of career information that are pertinent to their academic areas (for example, a list of job titles that graduates of the department are entering)

- Obtaining a list of jobs that graduates in their majors have obtained

- Establishing a small career resource library in their offices so that they can share with students firsthand information that is frequently requested

- Taking part in advisor training sessions that review or expand career-related expertise

When academic advisors use any of the career information delivery methods described, they are adding an important dimension to their advising. Students come to advisors with many academic concerns, some of which include career-related issues. Any career information advisors provide or any referral advisors make will enhance and expand their advising interactions with students.

Career Resources for Advising Offices

It is important for advisors to consider what career-related information they use regularly with students in their offices so that these resources are readily available. Information tailored to the needs of the students they advise will ensure its use. Business advisors, for example, might want to keep abreast of career information provided in the *Wall Street Journal* or other business-related publications. Advisors working with undecided students will want to use information resources that cover a broader spectrum of career-related topics. Additional general information resources might also be useful in advising centers or departmental advising offices.

Listed next are some suggestions for resources advisors might consider using when the situation warrants it. These are the types of resources that advisors can use to help students integrate or pull together all the information they have collected. They can provide additional information if gaps are detected during the integrative process. Campus career resource personnel can provide additional suggestions.

- A printed copy of the most recent version of the *Occupational Outlook Handbook*
- A printed copy of *The O*NET Dictionary of Occupational Titles*
- A printed copy of the *Dictionary of Holland Occupational Codes*
- A list of career-related Internet addresses that are targeted to their particular students
- A list of the institution's majors they work with, organized by Holland codes (or any other system that is used)
- A list of work values
- A list of work skills and job competencies relevant to their academic advising areas
- Curricula sheets of majors relevant to the advising area, with curricula on one side and related occupational information on the other
- Other career-related information handouts tailored to their advising areas
- A list of alumni who have graduated in the majors related to the advising areas to whom (after gaining permission) students can be referred for information

- Other career-related commercial printed materials relevant to the academic areas

- A referral form to the career services offices on campus with a checklist of the services available

Summary

Many of the methods and techniques used in academic advising are used in career advising as well. Certain areas of knowledge, such as learning about occupational information resources, however, need to be expanded. There are many methods for presenting career information, assessment, and planning. These include group advising, career courses, computerized career guidance systems, and the many resources on the Internet. Although advisors are not directly involved in career assessment tools, such as personality inventories, some knowledge of what they are and what they measure can be helpful when referring students to the career resources on campus. Suggested career resources for advising offices are also offered. The advisor's role is not to become a "career counselor" or test giver but to better understand the academically related career concerns that students present and the resources that are available to assist them in their academic planning and decision making. By becoming knowledgeable about career resources and where they can be used appropriately, advisors enhance the quality of their career-advising approaches.

7

FUTURE CHALLENGES

Academic advisors must be in tune with the remarkable changes unfolding in today's work world. The workplace today is undergoing significant changes just as earth-shaking as those of the Industrial Revolution. Many factors influence this evolving workplace and the workers who participate. Why should academic advisors be interested in the future from a career-advising perspective? One of the missions of higher education is to prepare future citizens and the nation's future workforce. Advising is a key factor in helping students use their college years preparing to become educated persons and productive workers. It is important to anticipate how society, higher education, and our future students might change.

Cascio (2000) describes a new workplace reality in which the psychological contract that binds workers and organizations to each other has been revised. For example, where we once had stability, we now have change and uncertainty. Where we once had linear career growth, we now have multiple careers. Where we once had standard work patterns, we now have flexible work. Economic conditions from the time students enter college until the time they graduate may change dramatically. Downsizing, reengineering, globalization, and organizational structures have changed the realities of the old workplace.

Workplace Trends

The *Futurist* ("Trends," 2003) describes projected work trends in the twenty-first century. "The half-life of an engineer's knowledge today is only 5 years; in 10 years, 90% of what an engineer knows will be available on the computer. In electronics, fully half of what a student learns as a freshman is obsolete by his or her senior year" (p. 35). For many professions and businesses, the sheer size of the body of knowledge required to excel will foster specialization. "The fast pace of technological change makes old careers obsolete, even as new ones open up to replace them" (p. 37).

The U.S. Department of Labor makes projections about the future labor force, work sites, occupations, the education and training that will be needed, and job openings. These projections are made for a ten-year period but are frequently updated (*Occupational Outlook Handbook [OOH], 2004–2005*). The most current ones are listed here:

Labor Force. The size and composition of the labor force is determined by population, that is, people who are working or looking for work. The workforce will continue to become more diverse. Hispanics will account for the greatest increase, but Asians will continue to be the fastest growing group. By 2012, White non-Hispanics will remain the largest group in the labor force at 65 percent. The number of women will grow at a faster rate than men. The number of primary working-age workers between 25 and 54 years old will decline, while workers 55 and older will increase (due to large numbers of Baby Boomers).

Employment. Total employment is expected to increase to 165 million by 2012. Changes in consumer demand, technology, and many other factors will contribute to the changing employment structure in the U.S. economy.

Work Sites. The long-term shift from goods-producing to service-providing employment is expected to continue. Over the next ten-year period, service-providing industries are expected to account for approximately 22 percent of new wage and salary jobs. These include education and health services; professional and business services; information; leisure and hospitality; trade; transportation and utilities; financial activities; government; and other nongovernment services. Education and health services are projected to grow faster and add more new jobs than any other sector.

Goods-producing industries are projected to experience slow growth over the next decade. These include construction; manufacturing; agriculture, forestry, and fishing; and mining. Demand for new housing and an increase in road, bridge, and tunnel construction will account for the bulk of job growth in the construction sector. Employment in agriculture and mining is expected to decrease due to advancements in technology.

Occupations. Expansion of service-providing industries is expected to continue, creating demand for many occupations. Projected job growth will vary among major occupational groups. Professional and related occupations will grow the fastest and add more jobs than any other major occupational group. Office and administrative support, farming, and production will show the slowest growth.

Education and Training. Education is essential for getting a high-paying job. In fact, for all but one of the fifty highest-paying occupations, a college degree or higher is the most significant source of education and training. (Air traffic controller is the only occupation for which this is not the case.) Among the twenty fastest-growing occupations, a bachelor's or associate's degree is the most significant source of education and training.

Total Job Openings. Job openings stem from both employment growth and replacement needs. Replacement needs arise as workers leave occupations. Some transfer to other occupations, while others retire, return to school, or quit to assume household responsibilities. Replacement needs are projected to account for 60 percent of the job openings in the next decade.

Advisors should have a print copy of the *Occupational Outlook Handbook (OOH)* in their offices or bookmark its Web site (http://www.bls.gov/oco) on their office computers. The *OOH* is an excellent source for the information quoted here and for the ease with which 822 detailed occupational descriptions can be accessed. Since most students will not be familiar with the *OOH*, advisors might recommend they bookmark it on their computers as well.

The changing composition of the workforce has always affected the need for new products and services. Aging populations, for example, create a need for health care. As indicated earlier, the future workforce will be more balanced in gender, ethnicity, and age. The new era of economic globalization is a result of the inexpensive, rapid flow of information technology. The changing nature of work tasks and processes has caused greater emphasis on retraining and lifelong learning.

Higher Education Trends

The many trends that prognosticators have suggested for higher education don't apply directly to career advising, but certain trends can indirectly affect how students access information and how campus services might be affected.

Morrison, Ericson, and Kohler (1995, p. 2) identified some critical trends affecting higher education and its students. Some of the economic trends they cite include:

- Corporate downsizing
- Lower wages for new graduates
- Increasing employer requirements for international skills (languages)
- Increasing needs for multiple degrees
- Increased demands for job placement
- Increased globalization

Other trends that are predicted to have an impact on higher education include:

Collaboration. Universities are forced to think along corporate lines now more than ever. To be more competitive, they have increased offerings in vocational certification and distance education programs (Conway, 2003). They have also increased their interest in partnerships with the business world. These partnerships might provide opportunities for internships and employment for students.

Changing Demographics. There is a major shift in the type of student entering higher education. In some institutions traditional-age youth are being replaced by an older population seeking a college education (Conway, 2003). "The average work life in the future will consist of six or seven different careers carried out sequentially. Life-long learning is becoming a necessity rather than the enrichment opportunity it may have been in the past" (Kovel-Jarboe, 2000, p. 2). Some of the changes in the student population that will be seen in the next decade are listed by Brint (2002):

- By 2012 there will be 18 million more students than today.
- Nineteen percent more will be in public institutions, 16 percent more in private institutions, and 11 percent more in community colleges.
- Students will be more racially and ethnically diverse.
- There will be more women than men (57 percent).
- More students will be in financial need.
- There will be more part-time, older students.
- All will be technologically literate.

Student Needs. There has been a major rethinking of student needs. Institutions that address the need to improve their academic and vocational offerings, both in traditional classes and at a distance, will fare better in the future (Conway, 2003). The growing diversity among students affects both educational planning and practice. Changes in academic and student services will be made to accommodate these changing student populations (Kramer, 2003).

Instructing Versus Learning. There is an increasing shift from an instruction to a learning paradigm. There is more focus on how students learn, by looking at various learning styles and multiple intelligences and designing learning environments based on these principles (Conway, 2003). Many questions are being asked about curriculum; how we teach and learn; about what experiences are essential to the educated person; and about the appropriate balance between education for a career and education for its own sake (Kovel-Jarboe, 2003).

Technological Changes. The rate at which new technologies are penetrating every facet of daily life can be expected to increase. Institutions will adapt to changing technologies by moving away from site-based delivery of education to more flexible, learner-selected options (Kovel-Jarboe, 2000).

Consumerism. Students and their parents today seek quality and accountability in their educational experiences. Customer satisfaction is as important today as are the traditional measures of academic quality (that is, size of libraries, staff-to-student ratios, number and size of grants). The student as consumer is a widely tolerated reality in many institutions. Kirp (2004) laments the "commercialization of higher education" through which multiple "constituencies" such as students, donors, corporations, and politicians promote their own visions of what the institution should be (p. 4).

The rising cost of a college education is raising questions about the value of a degree. Parents are asking during orientation about the services that will be available to their students, including career services. Advisors occasionally experience the wrath of a student or parent who is not satisfied that they are getting their "money's worth."

Implications for Students

Students entering this new workplace must be aware of how organizational structures are changing and the impact this has on job descriptions and requirements. They need to acquire the work and life skills to compete in this knowledge-based economy and adapt to technologies that are continually evolving. Some cognitive skills, such as abstract thinking, problem solving, communication, and collaboration, are more important than ever in this new work environment (May, 1995).

It is predicted that future generations of workers will lack both basic and specialized skills that will be needed in the future workplace. A survey of colleges found that enrollment in key courses for computer science majors, for example, decreased 10–30 percent (May, 2004).

Levy and Murnane (2004) discuss how computers are changing the employment scene by enhancing productivity in many jobs while at the same time eliminating other positions. A report by the National Research Council (NRC) (1999) lists information technology skills that are important in the workplace today. They include setting up a personal computer and using a number of applications such as word processing and spreadsheet programs. Although today most students learn these skills in school, the NRC stresses the need to acquire unmeasured skills that are the intellectual capabilities needed to be fluent with information technology. These include sustained reasoning, managing complexity, testing a solution, collaborating, and communicating to other audiences. Along with emphasizing the acquisition of basic computer skills, advisors must impress upon students the importance of developing the skills related to problem solving and complex communication.

Today's college students also need to understand the skills needed in a "hyper-human" economy (Samson, 2004, p. 41). They need to learn how to extract meaning from specific information; anticipate and creatively solve problems; see the big picture while focusing on individual needs; be able to troubleshoot technical and database problems, to name a few. Samson suggests that "if a form of work takes creativity, goal-focus, ethical behavior, responsibility, and social skills, it's likely to have a future" (p. 43). Emphasizing how students can acquire marketable skills through coursework and other college activities and resources is one task by which advisors can have a tremendous impact.

Acquiring Competencies for the Future

The U.S. Secretary of Labor commissioned a report to determine the skills and competencies that will be needed to succeed in this new century. The Secretary's Commission on Achieving Necessary Skills (SCANS) (2000) outlines both fundamental skills and workplace competencies. The basic skills listed in the report include reading, writing, mathematics, listening, and speaking. Thinking skills include creative thinking, decision making, problem solving, seeing things in the mind's eye, knowing how to learn, and reasoning. Students must develop the personal qualities of responsibility, self-esteem, sociability, self-management, and integrity/honesty. The SCANS committee also identified five workplace competencies in the areas of resources, interpersonal, information, systems, and technology.

SCANS has focused on the important aspect of education, "learning a living" since a high-performance workplace requires workers who have a solid foundation in basic skills as well as in the competencies mentioned above. Advisors can share lists of these competencies with students so that students can estimate their strengths and weaknesses in these areas. (The SCANS competencies can be found at http://www.academicinnovations.com/scans.html.) Advisors can help students determine what competencies and skills they need to learn or strengthen. For example, under "Systems," future workers will need to "know how social, organizational, and technological systems work and can operate them effectively" (SCANS, 2000, p. 3). Advisor and student can determine what specific courses will provide the expertise suggested in that competency and schedule accordingly.

Knotts (2002) emphasizes the value of liberal arts core courses for providing the skills needed in this "new economy." Economist Robert Allen (as quoted by Knotts) indicates that "new-style organizations put a premium on workers who can relate models to real situations, work well with other members of a management team or with clients, and who can speak and write effectively" (p. 27). Knotts lists the skills that are part of a liberal education:

Core Liberal Arts Skills

- Written communications
- Oral communication
- Creativity
- Critical thinking
- Theoretical thinking

Research Design Skills

- Data collection
- Hypothesis development
- Questionnaire construction
- Issues of validity and reliability

Data Analysis Skills

- Qualitative analysis
- Quantitative analysis
- Descriptive statistics
- Hypothesis testing
- Cross-tabular analysis
- Bivariate statistics
- Multivariate statistics

Computer Application Skills

- Spreadsheet applications
- Social science statistical software
- Geographic information systems software

General Business Skills

- Accounting
- Finance
- Management

Knotts states that advisors are uniquely positioned to help students develop personal, educational, and career goals. By stressing the importance of developing the skills listed, advisors can help students prepare for the complex marketplace they are about to enter.

Generational Differences

One area that demonstrates how students are changing in their perceptions of the workplace and their place in it is the study of generational differences. Although it is dangerous to stereotype individuals within a generation, certain characteristics seem to appear. Students' values and attitudes toward work are formed by the unique perspectives that their generation has developed and how this ultimately affects their decisions about how and where they work. Students and workers from each generation bring with them their own distinctive histories, work habits, work ethics, and work values. These perspectives were shaped by the unique experiences, trends, and events that took place during each generation's formative years.

Most academic advisers on today's campuses are Boomers (born 1946–1960) or Generation Xers (born 1960–1980). Many students are of the Millennial generation (born 1980–2000). Older students may be either Boomers or Gen Xers, or even from the Traditional generation (born 1925–1945). Boomers tend to be optimistic, competitive team workers and like to pursue personal gratification.

They are uncomfortable with conflict but are willing to "go the extra mile" (Zemke, Raines, & Filipczak, 2000, p. 76). Some Boomer advisors may have very different perspectives than their students about work values, habits, and ethical behavior. At times this may create communication problems when working with Gen Xers or Millennials (Gordon & Steele, 2005).

Generation X and the Millennial generation will have a major impact on the future workplace. These two generations thrive on challenge and opportunity. They may have different ideas from Boomers about authority, management expectations, patience, time, and dress in the office. They are very much into lifelong learning and how it can continuously prepare them for their next big career move ("Trends," 2003). Since they grew up with technology, they are well prepared for the high-tech world. The traditional-age college generation today is mostly made up of Millennials. This is the first generation to enter the new knowledge economy in which it grew up. As this generation enters the workforce, they will bring with them their appreciation for diversity, multitasking capabilities, and technological savvy (Lancaster & Stillman, 2002).

Saveri and Falcon (2000) discuss the intergenerational issues that are taking place today and will have an even greater impact in the future workforce. Differences in work styles, sense of timing and space, meaning in work, and needs will be difficult to generalize across the workforce. Age cohorts can help bridge the cultural gap created by social, cultural, and technological backgrounds.

Implications for Advisors

Advisors must assume responsibility, not only for staying current in their disciplines, but in the dynamic changes that are taking place in many types of work environments that their students will enter. Since most academic majors do not lead to a specific occupation, choosing a career path involves much more than the acquisition of academic knowledge. It may mean, for example, carefully selecting coursework outside of students' disciplines that provides the practical expertise that will help them succeed in a competitive marketplace. Organizations want employees who can fit into their missions and goals. This means "performing multiple jobs simultaneously or in sequence, designing or improving the efficiency of work processes, and sharing and cultivating the company's values" (May, 1995, p. 2). Students need to be aware that the tasks involved in specific jobs will not remain the same or be as enduring as in the past.

The knowledge and skills that career advisors must use in their work with students have changed along with most other professions. For example, advisors need to expand their knowledge of changes and trends in higher education and the workplace, the changing competencies needed for future employment in the discipline they are advising, the career-advising needs of diverse student populations, and the importance of continually updating their knowledge of their campus's career services. Although basic advising skills seldom change, technological advancements will require they learn new skills in this area. New ways of thinking must be incorporated into advisors' daily encounters with students and in nourishing their own professional development. This has great implications for advisor training and development programs as new information and techniques are evolving.

More specifically, academic advisors who assume responsibility for assisting students in career exploration and decision making will need to continually update their knowledge of career information and refine their career-advising skills. Career advisors can stay current in this area by reading, updating through the Internet, having discussions with colleagues, and engaging in professional development opportunities.

Career-Advising Research

Two of the areas on which Toman (2000) predicts that future career development research and practices will focus are the career decision needs of diverse students and an emphasis on advancing theory and practice. She suggests that more contextual research using case studies, longitudinal, narrative, and qualitative approaches is needed to complement the already highly developed use of quantitative designs.

The need for research in academic advising has been well documented (Frost, 1991; Gordon, 1998; Habley, 2000; McGillin, 2000). In McGillin's (2000) review of the research on academic advising topics, she found that advisors have not recognized career advising to be as significant as their advisees do and questioned their own ability to help students acquire decision-making skills. A recent study asked academic advisors what they considered the most important from a list of advising research topics (Padak, Kuhn, Gordon, Steele, & Robbins, 2005), and not one advisor selected career advising. Perhaps some advisors think that enough is known already about this aspect of advising or are not aware of its importance and influence on students. There are still many unanswered questions, however, about how and when advisors should broach the subject of careers with their students and how effective they are in this area. A few simple questions that might be asked include:

- How do advisors define career advising?
- How do advisors perceive their responsibility to "career advise"?
- What different models for career advising currently exist? How can they be improved?
- What career concerns do advisors hear most frequently from students?
- What types of students benefit most from career advising?
- What do students know about their own career development and how it progresses?
- What do advisors know about career development, career information, and career decision making?
- What are the most effective methods for broaching career exploration with students?

- What are the most common tools used by advisors in career advising?
- What are some career-advising outcomes that are important to students? To advisors?
- How and when are career-advising knowledge and skills provided in advisor training programs?

The list could go on and on. As advisors consider possible research projects, the possibilities for studies on this topic are unlimited.

Summary

Parmer and Rusk (2003) constructed a vision for career counseling using the metaphor of "cocoon maintenance" or being able to "see outside the walls of our impermeable cocoons" (p. 26). They suggest that in order to become a butterfly, the profession needs to think in new, creative ways. For example, all students should be considered diverse, that is, all advising should be from a "culturally relative perspective" (p. 29). There is no better time than now for some advisors to break out of the career-advising cocoon they have lived in for so long. Students need all the help they can get as they enter today's complex, competitive workplace.

Some areas where advisors can influence students through career advising include:

- Helping students gather and interpret complex educational and career information related to the work world of the future
- Helping them become career strategists, not just planners
- Helping them develop contextual and portable skills
- Helping them develop the ability to negotiate school and work environments
- Helping them develop contingency plans for changes
- Impressing upon them the need to set realistic and measurable personal, academic, and career goals

- Referring them with personally focused intent, rather than generically

CAS Standards Revisited

In Chapter 1, a checklist was presented (Checklist 1.1) of career-advising areas that advisors could use as an evaluative tool. Advisors can now examine this checklist (presented as Checklist 7.1) again to determine if their career knowledge has broadened and their career-advising practices have increased as a result of practicing some of the tenets described in these pages.

It is up to each advisor to decide if he or she wants to stay current in our complex, unpredictable work world or be uninterested, complacent, or uninvolved. As Charles Darwin said, "It is not the strongest species that survive, nor the most intelligent, but the ones most responsive to change." Advisors must be ready for the inevitable changes that will bring future challenges not only to their students' workplace, but to their own work environment as well.

Checklist 7.1   Career-Advising Questions Revisited

As an academic advisor I am now discussing with students:

____ The characteristics of the work environment they prefer at this point and why these characteristics are appealing to them

____ Possible career fields based on students' interests as expressed through choice of major or through other strong areas of interest

____ Possible career fields based on students' work values or what students say is important in their work lives

____ Possible career fields in which students' strongest abilities and skills would be used to their fullest advantage

____ How to identify students' knowledge, skills, and accomplishments from their formal education, work experience, community service, and volunteer experiences

____ Where and how students can acquire this essential knowledge and develop these skills if they do not have enough relevant experiences

____ How what they are learning in the classroom can be used in future work tasks, habits, and attitudes as well in life tasks

____ How the world of work is continually changing and how students can develop the skills needed to successfully enter and thrive in a variety of work environments

____ The importance of acquiring while in college technological skills essential to students' future employment

____ How students can begin to plan the steps they will need to take to search for a job after graduation, or the steps needed to plan for advanced education

____ How students can document the knowledge, skills, and accomplishments they have already acquired in a résumé format and what they can do to strengthen their general marketability

Source: Based on the "career choices" domain of the CAS standards (Council for the Advancement of Professional Standards for Higher Education, 2005).

Appendix A

Useful Career-Advising Web Sites

America's Career Information Network — http://wwwacinet.org/acinet

America's Job Bank — http://www.ajb.org

America's Service Locator — http://www.servicelocator.org

Career Choices — http://www.academic innovations.com/report.html

Career Key — http://www.careerkey.org

CareerScope — http://www.vri.org

Career Voyages — http://www.careervoyages.gov

Choices CT — http://www.bridges.com/usa/product/choices

Classification of Instructional Programs — http://nces.ed.gov/pub/2002/cip/2000

DISCOVER Guidance System — http://www.act.org/discover

ERIC Center for Assessment — http://www.searcheric.org

Federal disability resources — http://www.disabilityinfo.gov

Focus II Interactive System — http://www.focuscareer.com

The Futurist — http://www.wfs.org/futurist.htm

Jist (publisher) — http://www.jistworks.com

Keirsey Character Sorter — http://www.keirsey.com

Monster Campus — http://campus.monster.com

Myers-Briggs Type Indicator	http://www.capt.org
My Road	http://www.myroad.com
NACADA National Clearinghouse	http://www.nacada.ksu.edu
Occupational Outlook Handbook (OOH)	http://www.bls.gov/ocox
Occupational Outlook Quarterly (OOQ)	http://stats.bls.gov
O*Net (Occupational Information Network)	http://online.onetcenter.org
SCANS competencies	http://www.academicinnovations.com/scans.html
Self-Directed Search	http://www.self-directed-search.com
SIGI Plus	http://www.valparint.com
Standard Occupational Classification (SOC)	http://stats.bls.gov/soc
StrengthQuest	http://www.strengthquest.com
System of Interactive Guidance *(SIGI)*	http://valparint.com
Tests in Print	http://www.unl.edu/buros
U.S. Census	http://www.census.gov
U.S. Department of Labor	http://www.doleta.gov
U.S. Labor Market Information system	http://www.careeronestop.org
U.S. National Center for Education Statistics	http://nces.ed.gov/pubsearch
Volunteers and service	http://www.servenet.org
Women's Bureau Clearinghouse	http://www.dol.gov/wb

Appendix B

Case Studies for the 3-I Process

INQUIRE

Walt

Walt is a first-year student who is undecided about a major. He is in his advisor's office because he doesn't know what courses to schedule for his next semester. Up to now, he hasn't worried too much about choosing a major, but he's beginning to see how scheduling between the two or three ideas he has might buy him time. He wants to know how much longer he has before the college makes him choose. He thinks he should probably look into the three majors he is considering but so far hasn't the vaguest idea where to start. How will you advise him?

Caitlyn

Caitlyn entered the university as a nursing major. She has always wanted to be a nurse and volunteered in a hospital all through high school. However, she received notice a month ago that her application into the nursing program was rejected. She thinks this was because her low chemistry grades brought down her GPA. She has been depressed since receiving the letter and has difficulty accepting her situation. She has considered dropping out of college. She is totally lost in considering her next steps. How will you advise her?

INFORM

Jamal

Jamal is beginning his sophomore year as a business major and must designate a primary study area within the business curriculum. He indicates he chose business because his family strongly recommended it and he is eager to get a well-paying job after college. Although he hasn't taken enough courses in the business specialty areas to know which ones he prefers, he is considering either marketing or finance. He realizes he needs a great deal of information at this point. How will you advise him?

Amy

Amy is approaching the end of her junior year as a history major. She is beginning to realize that she needs information about job possibilities and the job search process. She has found some information on the Internet about jobs related to a history major but she wants to broaden her search to other areas. She is also thinking about public relations or teaching history. How will you advise her?

INTEGRATE

Sasha

Sasha is a senior who is graduating at the end of this semester as a computer science major. She has just learned that her family is moving back to India. She is torn, because she was counting on staying in the United States (she was born here), but she wants to be with her family. She has had several excellent job offers but is not sure which company would be the best for her. She has also thought about seeking a position as a computer specialist in India. How will you advise her?

Robert

Robert has been an outstanding athlete at the university and is starting his senior year as a physical education major. He is beginning to realize that his dream of becoming a professional baseball player is not going to happen. He is not sure how he will use his degree but knows he wants to work in the fitness or coaching areas. He has done considerable research in these two areas and has talked to many people. He feels he is so overloaded with information, he can't come to any decision. How will you advise him?

References

Abelman, R., & Molina, A. (2001). Style over substance revisited: A longitudinal analysis of intrusive intervention. *NACADA Journal, 21*(1&2), 32–39.

ACT, Inc. (1995). *WorkKeys*. Iowa City, IA: Author.

ACT, Inc. (2001). *World-of-Work Map*. Iowa City, IA: Author.

ACT, Inc. (2004). *The status of academic advising: Findings from the ACT Sixth National Survey*. NACADA Monograph Series, No. 10. Manhattan, KS: National Academic Advising Association.

American Counseling Association (ACA). (2005). *Professional counselors helping people*. Retrieved July 20, 2005, from http://www.counseling.org/Content/Navigationmenu/RESOURCES/PROFESSIONALCO

Amundson, N., Harris-Bowlsbey, J., & Niles, S. (2005). *Essential elements of career counseling: Processes and techniques*. Upper Saddle River, NJ: Prentice Hall.

Banta, T. W., Hansen, M. J., Black, K. E., & Jackson, J. E. (2002). Assessing advising outcomes. *NACADA Journal, 22*(1), 5–14.

Bates, A. W., & Poole, G. (2003). *Effective teaching with technology in higher education*. San Francisco: Jossey-Bass.

Begley, P. T., & Johnson, J. (2000). Academic advising and living the examined life: Making the case for a values perspective. *NACADA Journal, 21*(1&2), 8–14.

Betz, N. E. (2004). Contributions of self-efficacy theory to career counseling: A personal perspective. *Career Development Quarterly, 52*(4), 340–354.

Betz, N. E., & Hackett, G. (1986). Applications of self-efficacy theory to understanding career choice behavior. *Journal of Social & Clinical Psychology, 4*, 279–289.

Bluestein, D. L. (1992). Applying current theory and research to practice. *Career Development Quarterly, 41*, 174–184.

Boer, P. M. (2001). *Career counseling over the Internet*. Mahwah, NJ: Lawrence Erlbaum Associates.

Brint, S. (Ed.). (2002). *The future of the city of intellect*. Stanford, CA: Stanford University Press.

Brooks, J. E. (1995). Guide to developing a successful career course. *Journal of Career Planning and Employment, 55*(3), 29–31.

Brown, D. (1995). A values-based model for facilitating career transitions. *Career Development Quarterly, 44,* 4–11.

Brown, D. (2000). Theory and the school-to-work transition: Are the recommendations suitable for cultural minorities? *Career Development Quarterly, 48*(4), 370–375.

Brown, D. (2002). *Career information, career counseling, and career development* (8th ed.). Boston: Allyn & Bacon.

Buckingham, M., & Clifton, D. O. (2001). *Now, discover your strengths.* New York: Free Press.

Butler, E. R. (1995). Counseling and advising: A continuum of services. In R. E. Glennen & F. N. Vowell (Eds.), *Academic advising as a comprehensive campus process.* NACADA Monograph No. 2, pp. 107–114. Manhattan, KS: National Academic Advising Association.

Campbell, T. A., & Campbell, D. E. (1997). Faculty student mentor programs: Effects on academic performance and retention. *Research in Higher Education, 38,* 727–742.

Carter, R. T. (1991). Cultural values: A review of empirical research and implications for counseling. In D. Brown, L. Brooks, & Associates, *Career choice and development* (2nd ed., pp. 75–120). San Francisco: Jossey-Bass.

Cascio, W. F. (2000). The changing world of work: Preparing yourself for the road ahead. In J. M. Kummerow (Ed.), *New directions in career planning and the workplace* (pp. 3–31). Palo Alto, CA: Davies-Black.

Chickering, A. W., & Reisser, L. (1993). *Education and identity* (2nd ed.). San Francisco: Jossey-Bass.

Chung, Y. B., & Gfroerer, M. (2003). Career coaching: Practice, training, professional and ethical issues. *Career Development Quarterly, 52*(2), 141–154.

Conway, G. P. (2003). *Higher education trends in the 21st century.* Retrieved June 12, 2005, from http://www.degreeinfo.com/article11_1.html

Coplin, W. D. (2003). *10 things employers want you to learn in college.* Berkeley, CA: Ten Speed Press.

Coscarelli, W. (1983). *Manual for the decision making inventory.* Columbus, OH: Marathon Publishing.

Council for the Advancement of Professional Standards for Higher Education. (2005). *Academic advising: CAS standards and guidelines.* Washington, DC: Author. CAS standards also available at http://nacada.ksu.edu/Clearinghouse/Research_Related/CASStandardsForAdvising.pdf

Creamer, D. G., & Creamer, E. G. (1994). Practicing developmental advising: Theoretical contexts and functional applications. *NACADA Journal, 14*(2), 17–24.

Crites, J. O. (1981). *Career counseling: Models, methods, and materials.* New York: McGraw-Hill.

Crookston, B. B. (1972). A developmental view of academic advising as teaching. *Journal of College Student Personnel, 13,* 12–17.

Daller, M. L., Creamer, E. G., & Creamer, D. G. (1997). Advising styles observable in practice: Counselor, scheduler, and teacher. *NACADA Journal, 17*(2), 31–38.

DeVaney, S. B., & Hughey, A. W. (2000). Career development of ethnic minority students. In D. A. Luzzo (Ed.), *Career counseling of college students* (pp. 235–252). Washington, DC: American Psychological Association.

Dewey, J. (1910). *How we think.* Boston: Heath.

Dinklage, L. B. (1968). *Decision strategies of adolescents.* Unpublished doctoral dissertation, Harvard University, Cambridge, MA.

Dodson, J. P., Chastain, G., & Landrum, R. E. (1996). Psychology seminar: Careers and graduate study in psychology. *Teaching in Psychology, 23,* 238–240.

Donnelly, N. (2005). Advisor Job Satisfaction Survey. Retrieved from https://surveys.ksu.edu/Survey/PublicReport?offeringId=39992.

Ducat, D. (2002). *Turning points: Your career decision-making guide* (2nd ed.). Upper Saddle River, NJ: Prentice Hall.

Encylopedia of careers and vocational guidance. (2001). New York: Ferguson.

Evans, N. J., Forney, D. S., & Guido-DiBrito, F. (1998). *Student development in college: Theory, research, and practice.* San Francisco: Jossey-Bass.

Farr, J. M., Ludden, L. L., & Shatkin, L. S. (2001). *Guide for occupational exploration (GOE).* Indianapolis, IN: JIST Works.

Frost, S. H. (1991). *Academic advising for student success.* ASHE-ERIC Higher Education Report No. 3. ERIC Clearinghouse on Higher Education. Washington, DC: George Washington University.

Gordon, V. N. (1981). The undecided student: A developmental perspective. *Personnel and Guidance Journal, 59,* 433–439.

Gordon, V. N. (1995). *The undecided college student: An academic and career advising challenge* (2nd ed.). Springfield, IL: Charles C Thomas.

Gordon, V. N. (1998). New horizons: Learning from the past and preparing for the future. *NACADA Journal, 18*(1), 5–12.

Gordon, V. N., & Sears, S. J. (2004). *Selecting a college major: Exploration and decision making* (5th ed.). Upper Saddle River, NJ: Prentice-Hall.

Gordon, V. N., & Steele, M. J. (2005). The advising workplace: Generational differences and challenges. *NACADA Journal, 25*(1), 26–30.

Gottfredson, G. D., & Holland, J. L. (1996). *Dictionary of Holland occupational codes* (3rd ed.). Odessa, FL: Psychological Assessment Resources.

Grites, T. J. (1979). *Academic advising: Getting us through the eighties.* AAHE-ERIC/Higher Education Research Report No. 7. Washington, DC: American Association for Higher Education.

Grites, T. J., & Gordon, V. N. (2000). Developmental academic advising revisited. *NACADA Journal, 20*(1), 5–11.

Habley, W. R. (2000). On a clear day-ja vu all over again. *NACADA Journal, 20*(1), 5–11.

Habley, W. R. (2004). *The status of academic advising: Findings from the Sixth National Survey.* NACADA Monograph, No. 10. Manhattan, KS: National Academic Advising Association.

Halasz, J. T., & Kempton, C. B. (2000). Career planning courses and workshops. In D. A. Luzzo (Ed.), *Career counseling of college students* (pp. 157–170). Washington, DC: American Psychological Association.

Hardesty, P. H. (1991). Undergraduate career course for credit: A review and meta-analysis. *Journal of College Student Development, 32,* 184–185.

Harrington, T., & O'Shea, A. (2003). *Career decision making system (CDMS)* (4th ed.). Circle Pines, MN: American Guidance Services.

Hartung, P. J., & Niles, S. G. (2000). Established career theories. In D. A. Luzzo (Ed.), *Career counseling of college students* (pp. 3–21). Washington, DC: American Psychological Association.

Hettich, P. I. (2005). *Connect college to career: Student guide to work and life transition.* Belmont, CA: Wadsworth.

Hitchings, W. E., & Retish, P. (2000). The career development needs of students with learning disabilities. In D. A. Luzzo (Ed.), *Career counseling of college students* (pp. 217–231). Washington, DC: American Psychological Association.

Holland, J. (1994). *Self-directed search (SDS).* Odessa, FL: Psychological Assessment Resources.

Holland, J. L. (1997). *Making vocational choices: A theory of vocational personalities and work environment* (3rd ed.). Odessa, FL: Psychological Assessment Resources.

Iaccarino, G. (2002). Computer-assisted career guidance systems. In D. A. Luzzo (Ed.), *Career counseling of college students* (pp. 173–190). Washington, DC: American Psychological Association.

Jurgens, J. C. (2000). The undecided student: Effects of combining levels of treatment on career certainty, career indecision, and client satisfaction. *Career Development Quarterly, 48*(3), 237–250.

Kirp, D. L. (2004). *Shakespeare, Einstein, and the bottom line: The marketing of higher education.* Cambridge, MA: Harvard University Press.

Kivlighan, D. M. (1990). Career group therapy. *Counseling Psychologist, 18,* 64–80.

Knotts, H. G. (2002). Rethinking liberal arts skills in the new economy. *NACADA Journal, 22*(1), 26–31.

Kolb, D. A. (1967). *The Learning Style Inventory: Technical manual.* Boston: McBer.

Kolb, D. A. (1981). Learning styles and disciplinary differences. In A. W. Chickering (Ed.), *The modern American college.* San Francisco: Jossey-Bass.

Kovel-Jarboe, P. (2000). *The changing contexts of higher education and four possible futures for distance education.* Retrieved September 12, 2004, from http://www.horizon.unc.edu/projects/issues/paperskovel.asp

Kramer, G. L. (2000). Advising students at different educational levels. In V. Gordon & W. Habley (Eds.), *Academic advising: A comprehensive handbook* (pp. 84–104). San Francisco: Jossey-Bass.

Kramer, G. L. (2003). *Student academic services.* San Francisco: Jossey-Bass.

Krumboltz, J. D. (Ed.). (1966). *Revolution in counseling: Implications for behavioral science.* Boston: Houghton-Mifflin, pp. 235–283.

Krumboltz, J. D. (1996). A learning theory of career counseling. In M. L. Savickas & W. B. Walsh (Eds.), *Handbook of career counseling theory and practice.* Palo Alto, CA: Davies-Black.

Kummerow, J. M. (Ed.). (2000). *New directions in career planning and the workplace* (2nd ed.). Palo Alto, CA: Davies-Black.

Lancaster, L., & Stillman, D. (2002). *When generations collide.* New York: Harper-Collins.

Leonard, M. (2004). Results of the National Survey on Tehnology in Academic Advising. *NACADA Journal, 24*(1&2), 24–33.

Leong, F.T.L. (1986). Counseling and psychotherapy with Asian Americans: Review of literature. *Journal of Counseling Psychology, 33,* 196–206.

Levy, F., & Murnane, R. J. (2004). *The new division of labor.* Princeton, NJ: Princeton University Press.

Luzzo, D. A. (2000). Career development of returning-adult and graduate students. In D. A. Luzzo (Ed.), *Career counseling of college students* (pp. 191–215). Washington, DC: American Psychological Association.

Luzzo, D. A. (2002). *Making career decisions that count: A practical guide* (2nd ed.). Upper Saddle River, NJ: Prentice Hall.

Mau, W.C.J. (2004). Cultural dimensions of career decision-making. *Career Development Quarterly, 53*(1), 67–77.

May, K. E. (1995). *Work in the 21st century: Implications for selection.* Retrieved September 25, 2004, from http://www.siop.org/tip/backissuesTIPDec95/may.html

Mayhall, J. L., & Burg, J. E. (2002). Solution-focused advising with the undecided student. *NACADA Journal, 22*(1), 76–81.

McCalla-Wriggins, B. (2000). Integrating academic advising and career and life planning. In V. Gordon & W. Habley (Eds.), *Academic advising: A comprehensive handbook* (pp. 162–176). San Francisco: Jossey-Bass.

McGillin, V. A. (2000). Current issues in advising research. In V. N. Gordon, W. R. Habley, and Associates, *Academic advising: A comprehensive handbook* (pp. 365–380). San Francisco: Jossey-Bass.

Mentoring Leadership and Resource Network. (2003). Retrieved April 29, 2005, from http://mentors.net

Miller, T. K. (Ed.). (1997). *The book of professional standards for higher education.* Washington, DC: Council for the Advancement of Standards in Higher Education.

Miller, B., & Woycheck, S. (2003). The academic implications of the Self-Directed Search and Holland's theory: A study of Kent State

University exploratory students. *NACADA Journal, 23*(1&2), 37–43.

Morrison, J. L., Ericson, J., & Kohler, B. (1995). *Critical trends affecting the future of higher education in Minnesota.* Retrieved September 12, 2004, from http://horizon.unc.edu/projects/seminars/SCUP.asp. Copyright Horizon site.

National Academic Advising Association (NACADA). (2004). *Statement on the concept of academic advising.* Retrieved October 7, 2004, from http://www.nacada.ksu.edu/definitions.htm

National Career Development Association (NCDA). (1997). *Guidelines for the use of the Internet for provision of career information and planning services.* Retrieved October 27, 2004, from http://www.ncda.org/about/polnet.html

National Center for Education Statistics (NCES). (2002). *Classification of instructional programs (CIP).* [online] Available: http://nces.ed.gov/pubsearch/pubsinfo

National Forum on Information Literacy. (2004). Retrieved January 7, 2005, from http://www.infolit.org/definitions/index.html

National Research Council (NRC). (1999). *Being fluent with information technology.* Washington, DC: National Academy Press.

Niles, S. G., & Harris-Bowlsbey, J. (2002). *Career development interventions in the 21st century.* Upper Saddle River, NJ: Prentice-Hall.

O'Banion, T. (1972). An academic advising model. *Junior College Journal, 42,* 62–64, 66–69.

O'Banion, T. (1994). Retrospect and prospect. *NACADA Journal, 14,* 117–119.

Occupational outlook handbook, 2004–2005. Indianapolis, IN: JistWorks.

O'Halloran, T. M., Fahr, A. V., & Keller, J. R. (2002). Career counseling and the information highway: Heeding the road signs. *Career Development Quarterly, 50*(4), 371–376.

Olson, G. T., & Whitman, P. D. (1990). *Career information delivery system inventory.* (Eric Document Service No. ED 326688).

*O*NET dictionary of occupational titles.* (2001). Indianapolis, IN: JistWorks.

Osipow, S., Carney, C., Winer, J., Yanico, B., & Koschier, M. (1997). *Career decision scale (CDS).* Odessa, FL: Psychological Assessment Resources.

Padak, G., Kuhn, T., Gordon, V., Steele, G., & Robbins, R. (2005). Voices from the field: Building a research agenda for academic advising. *NACADA Journal, 25*(1), 6–10.

Pardee, C. F. (1994). We profess developmental advising, but do we practice it? *NACADA Journal, 14*(2), 59–61.

Parmer, T., & Rusk, L. C. (2003). The next decade in career maintenance or metamorphosis? *Career Development Quarterly, 52*(1), 26–36.

Perry, W. G., Jr. (1999). *Forms of intellectual and ethical development in the college years.* San Francisco: Jossey-Bass.

Peterson, G. W., Lenz. J. G., & Sampson, J. P., Jr. (2003). The assessment of readiness for student learning in college. In G. L. Kramer & Associates, *Student academic services* (pp. 103–125). San Francisco: Jossey-Bass.

Peterson, G. W., Sampson, J. P., Jr., & Reardon, R. C. (1991). *Career development and services: A cognitive approach*. Pacific Grove, CA: Brooks/Cole.

Pope, M. (2000). A brief history of career counseling in the United States. *Career Development Quarterly, 48*(3), 194–211.

RAND Corporation. (2004). *The future at work: Trends and implications*. Retrieved September 14, 2004, from http://rand.org/publications/RB/RB5070

Reardon, R. C., Lenz, J. G., Sampson, J. P., & Peterson, G. W. (2000). *Career development and planning*. Belmont, CA: Wadsworth.

Reardon, R. C., & Lumsden, J. A. (2003). Career interventions: Facilitating strategic academic and career planning. In G. L. Kramer and Associates, *Student academic services* (pp. 167–185). San Francisco: Jossey-Bass.

Reardon, R. C., Lumsden, J. A., & Meyer, K. E. (2004). *The Florida State University Portfolio Program (CPP)*. Technical Report #35. Tallahassee, FL: Florida State University, Center for the Study of Technology in Counseling and Career Development.

Reed, C., Reardon, R., Lenz, J., & Leierer, S. (2001). Reducing negative thoughts with a career course. *Career Development Quarterly, 50,* 158–167.

Reinarz, A. G., & Ehrlich, N. J. (2002). Assessment of academic advising: A cross-sectional study. *NACADA Journal, 22*(2), 50–65.

Rudolph, F. (1962). *The American college and university: A history*. New York: Vintage Books.

Sampson, J., Peterson, G., Lenz, J., Reardon, R., & Saunders, D. (1996). *Career thoughts inventory*. Odessa, FL: Psychological Assessment Resources.

Sampson, J., Reardon, R., Peterson, G., & Lenz, J. (2003). *Career counseling and services: A cognitive information processing approach*. Belmont, CA: Wadsworth.

Samson, R. W. (2004). How to succeed in the hyper-human economy. *Futurist, 38*(5), 38–43.

Saveri, A., & Falcon, R. (2000). Planning for the 21st century workforce. In J. M. Kummerow (Ed.), *New directions in career planning and the workplace* (pp. 33–76). Palo Alto, CA: Davies-Black.

Savickas, M. L., & Walsh, W. B. (1996). *Handbook of career counseling theory and practice*. Palo Alto, CA: Davies-Black.

Schein, H. K., & Laff, N. S. (1997). Working with undecided students: A hands-on strategy. *NACADA Journal, 17*(1), 42–48.

Schein, H. K., Laff, N. S., & Allen, D. R. (2004). *Giving advice to students: A road map for college professionals*. NACAD Monograph Series, No. 11. Manhattan, KS: National Academic Advising Association.

Sears, S. J., & Gordon, V. N. (2002). *Building your career: A guide to your future* (3rd ed.). Upper Saddle River, NJ: Prentice-Hall.

Sharf, R. S. (1997). *Applying career development theory to counseling* (2nd ed.). Pacific Grove, CA: Brooks/Cole.

Smart, J. C., Feldman, K. A., & Ethington, C. A. (2000). *Academic disciplines: Holland's theory and the study of college students and faculty.* Memphis, TN: Vanderbilt University Press.

Sotto, R. R. (2000). Technological delivery systems. In V. N. Gordon & W. R. Habley and Associates, *Academic advising: A comprehensive handbook* (pp. 249–257). San Francisco: Jossey-Bass.

Steele, G. (2003). A researched-based approach to working with undecided students: A case study illustration. *NACADA Journal, 23*(1 & 2), 10–20.

Steele, G., Miller, M., Steele, M., & Kennedy, G. (2005). Letter to the editor: Campus perspectives on academic advising and technology. *NACADA Journal, 25*(1), 12–13.

Steele, M. J., & Gordon, V. N. (2001). Advising by e-mail: Some advisors' perceptions. *NACADA Journal, 21,* 88–91.

Sue, D. W., & Sue, D. (1990). *Counseling the culturally different* (2nd ed.). New York: Wiley.

Super, D. E. (1990). A life-span, life-space approach to career development. In D. Brown, L. Brooks, & Associates (Eds.), *Career choice and development: Applying contemporary theories to practice* (2nd ed., pp. 197–261). San Francisco: Jossey-Bass.

Super, D. E., & Bohn, M. J. (1970). *Occupational psychology.* Belmont, CA: Wadsworth.

Taylor, K. M., & Popma, J. (1990). Construct validity of the CD-MSE Scale and the relationship of CDMSE to vocational indecision. *Journal of Vocational Behavior, 37,* 17–31.

Tiedeman, D., & O'Hara, R. (1963). *Career development: Choice and adjustment.* New York: College Entrance Examination Board.

Toman, S. M. (2000). The identification of a career development research and practice agenda for the 21st century. In D. A. Luzzo (Ed.), *Career counseling of college students* (pp. 311–332). Washington, DC: American Psychological Association.

Trends in labor force and work. (2003). *Futurist, 37*(2), 35–39.

Tyler, L. (1953). *The works of the counselor.* New York: Appleton-Century-Crofts.

U.S. Secretary's Commission on Achieving Necessary Skills (SCANS). (2000). *What work requires of schools: A SCANS report for America 2000.* Washington, DC: U.S. Department of Labor.

Vernick, S. H., Reardon, R. C., & Sampson, J. P., Jr. (2002). *Process evaluation of a career course: A replication and extension.* Technical Report #31. Tallahassee, FL: Florida State University, Center for the Study of Technology in Counseling and Career Development.

Whiston, S. C., Sexton, T. L., & Lasoff, D. L. (1998). Career-interventions outcome: A replication and extension of Oliver and Spokane (1988). *Journal of Counseling Psychology, 45,* 150–165.

Wycoff, J. (1991). *Mindmapping: Your personal guide to exploring creativity and problem-solving.* New York: Berkley Books.

Zemke, R., Raines, C., & Filipczak, B. (2000). *Generations at work.* New York: AMACOM.

Zunker, V. G. (2001). *Career counseling: Applied concepts of life planning* (6th ed.). Belmont, CA: Wadsworth.

Index